GOD SAVED ME

GOD SAVED ME

PART OF GOD'S FAITH HARVEST

WYLIE COMP

WESTBOW
PRESS
A DIVISION OF THOMAS NELSON

WestBow Press books may be ordered through booksellers or by contacting:

WestBow Press
A Division of Thomas Nelson
1663 Liberty Drive
Bloomington, IN 47403
www.westbowpress.com
1-(866) 928-1240

ISBN: 978-1-4497-9206-0 (sc)
ISBN: 978-1-4497-9207-7 (e)

Library of Congress Control Number: 2013907110

Printed in the United States of America.

WestBow Press rev. date: 05/09/2013

GOD SAVED ME

. . . the Apostle Peter, having observed the Lord walking on the sea, bade Jesus to allow him to walk on the water and come to Him. Peter stepped out in faith and began to walk toward Christ. He took his eyes off Jesus and immediately he was afraid and began to slip beneath the surface. Peter cried out, Lord save me and Jesus stretched forth His hand and Peter was saved

Peter was saved and his testimony was immediately changed from Lord save me to "God saved me"

Every believer has this same testimony

DEDICATION

To Jo, . . . always there,
no matter the circumstance.
Thick and thin have new meanings
when considered with being there through it all.

ACKNOWLEDGEMENTS

Special acknowledgement and thanks to Rev. Richard Kimble-Gordon, Pastor of Gateway Christian Fellowship Church in Dover, UK. Richard provided valuable assistance in reviewing the original manuscript. His counsel in organizing some of the strategic categories brought clarity and understanding to the final preparation of *God Saved Me*. Richard's heart and concern is for the lost. As a quiet and humble servant of our Lord and Savior, Jesus Christ, Richard is an example to all who would take up the challenges of witnessing and outreach.

Special acknowledgement and thanks to Ed, Babette and Stephen Hosier, in Ozark, MO, who provided their personal assistance in producing the manuscript. They share the vision for this effort and the hope that *God Saved Me* will encourage believers at all levels.

Acknowledgements

FOREWORD

R ev. Wylie Comp has written one of the most comprehensive books on the subject of Christian witnessing that I have ever had the privilege of reading or reviewing. *God Saved Me* is written on a level that anyone can understand and use as a guide for becoming an effective Christian soldier in the Army of God.

We are living in a day and time when it becomes less and less popular, in our secular society, to stand up for Christ. Rev. Comp has not only addressed this as an issue, but has given a variety of approaches that anyone, who seriously wants to share Christ with an unbeliever, can find a suitable path for them to follow as they learn to carry out the great commission.

Not only is Rev. Comp's book thorough and interesting, I have personally witnessed his presentation of this material to a congregation in a series of meetings. After nearly 8 months has transpired, many in the congregation, as well as the pastor, continue to refer to the material and the presenter in very positive ways.

I would highly recommend this book, especially as the background for the seminar. The value of the seminar is the question and answer periods where witnessing scenarios, real or foreseen, can be discussed with input, not only from Rev. Comp, but from a number of believers. The camaraderie encourages witnessing not only in teams but as individuals in the workplace and the marketplace.

Dr. Gerald F. Terrebrood
Co-Director
Soul Impressions
Ozark, MO

CONTENTS

INTRODUCTION

Being saved is the most important part of anyone's life. But just being saved is not as fulfilling as knowing you are saved. Especially when you understand from, or even better, for, what you have been saved. And, letting others in on the process is something which every believer should become involved.

1971 was an extremely good year for the writer. This is the year he took on a new life changing dimension and became a born again Christian. Sharing that experience became a dominate force in his life: Simply letting those in his immediate surroundings know about the love of Christ and His sacrifice for all mankind.

God Saved Me has been written by someone called by God who, with His help, wrote these words to encourage believers to be aware of their position in Christ and be willing to prepare their minds and hearts for the challenges ahead. Then be available to participate in sharing the "Good News" whenever and with whomever God gives the opportunity.

In talking with others, believers and non-believers, it quickly becomes all too clear that for some, the idea of simply sharing one's faith is an uncomfortable undertaking at best. It is far too easy to side-step the God issue and allow the topic of the moment to monopolize our speech and even our thoughts. God's commandments have been compromised by situational ethics. It's not that we don't care, because we do. We are just not comfortable in sharing our faith. It's too personal and of course we cannot allow our feelings about our faith to make anyone uncomfortable, else we become known as some type of religious zealot.

We all know, or know of, folks who tread on being obnoxious about their sanctimonious position. We avoid them whenever and wherever possible so as to not be considered odd or abnormally consumed with our religion or personal interpretation of faith. It seems to be our position that by not participating in the process, we can eliminate the problem. Some are saying that after all, God will save whom He will and those who reject the truth will continue rejecting it no matter what we say.

There is some truth in that approach, but it does not address our true position in God's family of believers. If we cannot, or won't, get involved in telling others about God's plan for eternal security, who will?

In recent times, we have seen atrocities that go beyond description, performed in the name of a god that makes no provision for coexistence with any dissenters. Accept and convert or die. That does not leave any options or room for discussion. Some deranged cleric interprets words from a manuscript that is suspect at best and demands that every person in the world adhere to the "current interpretation" or be marked for death. To this, add numerous cults and isms which hold unusual if not similar positions and chaos reigns.

All "Ol' what's his name" (author's unaffectionate reference to Satan, Evil One, Lucifer, the Great Deceiver) has to do is get out of the way. Confusion and chaos will take their toll and those who should or would be telling the truth to a dying world, get the blame along with a good dose of frustration. It's time, way passed time, for Christians to take control of the moments God has given and be prepared to share the truth that lives within us: The truth that motivates our true thoughts about the reality of eternity and who will enjoy it.

David Mains made a very succinct statement in <u>The Rise of the Religion of Antichristism</u>, when he wrote, "Today believers are under attack from an enemy who personifies the evil of which . . . earlier conquerors were only a type. The threat is world-wide, but because national histories affect the battle between the spiritual kingdoms, North America is now a critical theater of conflict." [a]

For sure, there are those in the family of God that are in the world with their lights on at high beam, and with the truth in their hearts and on their lips. But for the most part, they are an exception, not a rule. So, the natural, if not obvious question is: What should I do? Revolution comes to mind, but revival is more appropriate. Old time revival should become "revival in our time"—but where to start? Here's a thought:

Throw a pebble into a pond and ripples result. Bigger pebble makes larger ripples. Problem comes when the ripples are consumed by the pond. There is no more evidence of the pebble and no influence can be observed on the surface. Keep throwing in pebbles and the result will be a pile of rocks and no more pond. Turn on a water faucet and not only are ripples produced, but the energy is continuous. Keep the water flowing and the pond will grow, even overflow its banks and have an impact on everything around it.

The big difference is not the faucet, but the water supply system. The faucet is connected to something bigger than itself and can utilize this larger source to continue the flow. Revival is like this. Think of yourself as a faucet. Draw a circle around your feet and stand in it. Plug into the power source (turn on the water) and make your circle larger. Increase the flow and your circle becomes even larger. More faucets, more ripples. Pretty soon the circles connect and the surface of the pond begins to dance. Revival!

Over simplification? Not really. After God created the pond He filled it and then He created us and put us in charge of the pond. In fact, He put us in charge of all the ponds and everything in and around them. There is a problem with ponds; they can become stagnant. Stirring the water helps but fresh water is required to keep the ponds alive. And a faucet is no help unless it is connected to a water supply and turned on. Think about it. We are all "faucets." And whether we are turned on or off, we need to be connected to a "source," if we are to ever have an "effect" on our pond.

A disconnected faucet won't work. It is still a faucet, but totally ineffective for the purpose to which it was designed. Hook it up to a water line and the potential for use is dramatically changed. If we, as believers, are to consider ourselves as faucets, we must be connected to "the source" and turned on to function as God intended. How do we do this?

That is the main purpose of this writing. Helping to implement a "how" is part of this author's calling. No one believer has an all-encompassing plan or process to get the family of God involved in telling the unsaved about the saving power of the Lord Jesus Christ and the eternal security that comes with allowing the Holy Spirit to enter in and assume control of our lives.

It is also important to note that there are several areas of outreach, witnessing and evangelism that require specific, if not major attention beyond what is discussed in this writing. Not the least of which is dealing with cults. In *the Psychological Structure of Cultism* chapter of his book, The Kingdom of the Cults, Walter Martin wrote, ". . . the belief systems of the cults are characterized by closed mindedness. They are not interested in a rational evaluation of the facts." [b] For this and other reasons, a Christian desiring to be involved in sharing God's truth with a cultist should, as a prerequisite, become acquainted with and be able to identify, not only the subtleties of confusion, but also the specifics of a misguided doctrine. Witnessing in this arena is a "special calling." Unless a major commitment to prayer, study and preparation can be made to this area of outreach, a believer would be encouraged to proceed with caution. Caution being the operative by-word here. Verbal fisticuffs with individuals caught-up in the throes of some misguided or misdirected understanding of God's truth for His creation will most certainly result in compromise.

Rules are also important, so far as they go in guiding society and assisting in the common good of those who are subordinate to them. God established a few rules of His own, which mankind has, at different times ignored or attempted to improve. The result, for the most part, has been a dismal failure. When obeyed, good rules enhance our lives and provide boundaries that guide our participation in life. A person filled with the Holy Spirit does not cease to believe in the commandments of God. That person reasonably accepts their position in God's forever family and through demonstrated faith can say that the condemnation of law, i.e., punishment for not being able to stay within the boundaries, has been done away by the redeeming power of the Blood of Jesus Christ.

One of the great spiritual leaders of modern time, Smith Wigglesworh, wrote in Ever Increasing Faith, "Does a man who is filled with the Spirit cease to keep the commandments? I simply repeat what the Spirit of God has told us [here], that this ministration of death, written and engraven in is DONE AWAY. The man who becomes a living epistle of Christ, written with the Spirit of the living God, has ceased to be an adulterer, or a murderer or a covetous man; the will of God is his delight. I love to do the will of God; there is no irksomeness to it; it is no trial to pray; no trouble to read the Word of God; it is not a hard thing to go to the place of worship. With the psalmist you say, 'I was glad when they said unto me, Let us go into the house of the Lord.'"

How does this new life work out? The thing works out because God works in you to will and to do of His own good pleasure (cf. Philippians 2.13). There is a great difference between a pump and a spring. The law is a pump, the Baptism is a spring. The old pump gets out of order, the parts perish, and the well runs dry. The letter killeth. But the spring is ever bubbling up and there is a ceaseless flow direct from the throne of God. There is life." [c]

The Church plays a significant role in the whole scheme of things associated with telling others about the salvation experience and what that means to us in today's world. And, no denomination has a corner on the market when it comes to evangelism and outreach. The Church in this example is akin to the First Century Church, AD, where believers, who were encumbered by religious dogmas, held to each other through the simple truth of the Gospel: Christ was born and lived among us, was crucified for our sin, rose from the dead on the third day to prove His point, and now represents us to God The Father and indwells us through the power of the Holy Spirit, so we can know we have eternal life.

Denominationalism can help with our individual interpretations of faith, but it cannot and does not alter the Gospel. Any form of ministry that diminishes or attempts to alter the pure truth of the Gospel is not where believers should be spending their time, energies or resources. Adopt any denominational theory you wish so long as it does not come against the foundational statement of faith enclosed and espoused by the Gospel message of Christ. We are not looking for converts to or for a specific church. We are looking for those who do not know the truth.

When we find them, or, as is oftentimes the case, they find us, we are to tell them the truth. If they accept the truth, it becomes our responsibility to nurture them and help them grow in their newfound faith. The Church is where this is best accomplished. And the Church is more effective as a body of believers, working together, (out of our salvation, not for it), toward the purposes to which we have been called by God. Baptist, Methodist, Presbyterian,

Lutheran, Episcopalian, Catholic, Pentecostal, Independent, non-denominational, or whatever label best fits our faith-walk, we are to be united by the truth that lives within us.

It is good to remember that ". . . you have been saved, through faith—and this not from yourselves, it is the gift of God—." [1] It's God's work. We are the laborers in His field, ". . . look at the fields! They are ripe for harvest." [2] Salvation is truly a "Faith Harvest."

CHAPTER ONE

EVANGELISM AND THE LOCAL CHURCH

Desire of Local Body to be Involved

Local Body Must Make Itself Available

Work Must be Grounded in the Local Body

"Lone Ranger" Evangelism Is Not Required

First Century Church / New Testament Church

Many Are Called . . . Few Respond

Fear and Confusion: Tools of the Devil

Where Are the Christians?

Hell is Promised to the Lost

Statement of Concern

Commitment to Each Other

Questions

Evangelism is a serious responsibility that has been assigned by God to local bodies of believers, and through them to individuals and ministries involved in sharing Christ with the lost. This responsibility cannot be shirked by leadership or specific entities which have been called to be involved with the concept of outreach to those in need of the truth. We live in a time where confusion and debauched life-styles are more prevalent than ever before. All Christ centered believers alive today should feel some responsibility toward getting the truth out to those desperately in need of knowing God's plan for His own.

Desire of the Local Body to be Involved

Reluctant participation in anything leaves a lot to be desired. If your heart isn't in it, the effort will be a burden and the reward will be less than anticipated. Let your imagination go and see if you can picture a local group of anything being involved in some program or process that requires participation without enthusiasm or desire. What do you see? Whatever comes to mind, it will involve boredom, bleakness, bad case of the blahs, and a little or a lot of "I don't wanna."

A while back (actually years ago, now) I was part of a church in Texas that was covenantly related to the work of preaching and teaching the Word of God. Their ministry involved multiple programs in an attempt to encourage as many folks as possible to grow in their faith and develop their lives around the will of God. They were committed to world evangelism and regularly held Missionary Emphasis Meetings and Seminars at the Church. On one such occasion an unusual situation developed.

Approaching the Church on a Sunday morning, during one of the Missionary Emphasis Meetings, I noticed a man and three children sitting on the ground near the particular entrance I was using. I stopped and inquired as to their plight. They told me they had been on a family outing and were on their way home when their van broke down. They had been walking for miles and had stopped here to rest before continuing with their journey toward their home in a nearby city. They had hoped someone might have given them a ride. Maybe even help them fix their van, but as yet no one had stopped or offered. I thought, what an opportunity. Our Church was packed full of believers from all around the country. A quick run up the hill and these folks would have all the help they would need. I gave them a box of the doughnuts I was taking to the meeting and asked them to come away from the roadside and wait a few minutes while I went to get some friends to help. They nodded in appreciation, moved away from the edge of the highway and I scurried up the hill to let those gathered at the Church know of the blessing God had placed on our doorstep.

When I reached the Church building the meeting had just started. A song-fest was in progress and here I came in glowing with the anticipation of being part of actually helping someone in need on this auspicious occasion. I located one of the Associate Pastors and told him about the folks at the bottom of the hill. I asked if he wanted me to make the announcement to the congregation, or if it was something he thought would be more appropriate if he made it. To my complete surprise he deferred to the Church's Business Manager who said now was not a good time to become involved in something like this. Now is not a good time, I asked? We're in the midst of a Missionary Emphasis Meeting; God has placed a needy family on our doorstep and now is not a good time? He said it was not the Church's policy to minister to every panhandler who came to the Church. When I explained the circumstances as I knew them, he deferred to the Senior Pastor.

I knew the Senior Pastor to be a compassionate man and was surprised when he agreed with the Business Manager's assessment of the situation. When I insisted that these folks were not panhandlers, but folks in need, he put me with the Associate Pastor with whom I had already visited. Following a brief exchange of alternatives the Associate Pastor asked me to wait a moment. When he came back he had a check made out to me for $20.00 and suggested I go back down the hill and do what I thought best for the man and his family. I was shocked and gave the check back to him. I sought out my own family and told them I was going to go and do what I could for the folks at the bottom of the hill. I was going to take them to their home in the nearby city, find out more about their more extended needs and be back as soon as possible.

All the while, I was thinking about all these "believers" coming together for a Missionary Emphasis Meeting around the idea of spreading the Gospel and helping people know the love of Jesus. God had placed an opportunity at the very door of the Church and the Church neither could nor would respond, for whatever rationale or reason.

I headed down the hill to collect the family and follow through with my word to them that I would go for help and be right back. Right back had turned into about thirty-five minutes or so. When I got back to where I had left them they were getting into a large yellow Cadillac. God had sent someone who would, when all of those who could were left uninformed about the opportunity. I smiled through the tears and thanked God for sending someone to do what could have been a wonderful blessing for all those gathered in His name on the pretense of doing His work. I went back to the Church, collected my family and headed home. Disappointment was one of my better feelings that day.

> Note: On our way home we passed by what was obviously a
> broken down van sitting alongside the road, right where the man
> told me they had left it. Two days later the van was gone.

Replace that picture with a group of believers who are sold out for God and willing to follow His instructions, and you will find enthusiastic participants who are filled with desire and looking to do the work to which they have been called.

The Word of God is ripe with instruction and examples as to what believers should do and how they should react to being the custodians of Christ's message to a lost and dying world. In his letter to Titus, Paul wrote, "Remind the people to be subject to rulers and authorities, to be obedient, *to be ready to do whatever is good*, (emphasis mine), to slander no one, to be peaceable and considerate, and to show true humility toward all men." [1] Being prepared and ready to share is high on the "how to" list in getting the truth that we have within us out for those who need to know. In his first epistle, Peter wrote, ". . . in your hearts set apart Christ as Lord. Always be prepared to give an answer to everyone who asks you to give the reason for the hope that you have. But do this with gentleness and respect." [2]

As believers, we need to be sensitive to the leading of the Holy Spirit. We should not be or become judgmental, and very important, we should not think more highly of ourselves than we should. (cf. Romans 12.3). It might have been possible, or even better, probable, that had the leadership of the church in Texas been more sensitive to the leading of the Holy Spirit and less quick to judge the condition of a stranger's heart, those who were assembled in the Lord's name and for His purpose, would have been blessed beyond description. The writer of Hebrews reminds all believers to "Keep on loving each other as brothers. Do not forget to entertain strangers, for by so doing some people have entertained angels without knowing it." [3]

The Apostle Peter declared that he was a witness to the sufferings of our Lord and Savior and that he would share in His glory when it is revealed. In his first epistle, recalling a truth reflected in the Book of Proverbs, he wrote, ". . . All of you clothe yourselves with humility toward one another, because 'God opposes the proud but gives grace to the humble.' Humble yourselves, therefore, under God's mighty hand, that He may lift you up in due time." [4]

Christ provided the example of a humble servant King which was written of by the writer of Hebrews. "So Christ also did not take upon Himself the glory of becoming a high priest. (He humbled Himself before man). But God said to Him, 'You are my Son; today I have become your Father.' And He says in another place, 'You are a priest forever, in the order of Melchizedek.'" [5] If we understand who Melchizedek was, we get a better idea of this example, which was placed in Scripture by inspiration of the Holy Spirit.

Melchizedek was a King of Salem, a contemporary of Abraham. He was not from the tribe of Levi and in fact pre-dated the patriarch Levi by two generations. The Torah and the Old Testament affirm that Melchizedek was a "priest of God Most High." [6] In the Psalms, King David refers to the future King of kings or Messiah as a "priest for ever after the order of Melchizedek." [7]

As believers, congregationally or individually, like Melchizedek, we are to serve one another. And we are to approach God on His terms. Christ humbled Himself before those to whom He ministered. He provided the example and gave us instructions as to how we should come to the throne of grace. "And when you pray, do not be like the hypocrites, for they love to pray standing in the synagogues and on the street corners to be seen by men. I tell you the truth, they have received their reward in full. But when you pray, go into your room, close the door and pray to your Father, who is unseen. Then your Father, who sees what is done in secret, will reward you. And when you pray, do not keep on babbling like pagans, for they think they will be heard because of their many words. Do not be like them, for your Father knows what you need before you ask Him." [8]

Matthew, the Apostle, recorded a most excellent example of what Christ said about us communicating with God. We know it as the Lord's Prayer. In actuality; it is a blueprint, an outline if you will, for mankind's prayers to God.

"After this manner therefore pray ye:

> Our Father which art in Heaven, Hallowed would be Thy name,
> Thy kingdom come, Thy will be done in earth, as [it is] in heaven.
> Give us this day our daily bread, and forgive us our debts,
>   as we forgive our debtors.
> And lead us not into temptation, but deliver us from evil:
> For Thine is the kingdom, and the power, and the glory, for ever.
> Amen." [9]

With the correct attitude toward communicating with God, about whatever it may be that we feel burdened to share with Him, or to just praise Him, it's also a good thing to have our thoughts organized and our hearts in the right place. Part of this commitment comes from being part of a body of believers who regularly come together to worship God and encourage one another in each other's individual walk. A requisite for this is for the local body of believers to have Word based, motivated, and quality oriented leaders that are faithful and teachable.

In Paul's second letter to Timothy, he wrote, ". . . be strong in the grace that is in Christ Jesus. And the things you have heard me say in the presence of many witnesses entrust to reliable men who will also be qualified to teach others." [10] Leadership that is developed around this understanding agrees with God's direction to get the Word out.

We all may know, or know of folks who claim to be a representative of the truth and that God has touched their life and now they are here to show us the way. There's a test for these folks: Who sent you? And we might want to confirm whether or not they have a teachable spirit. A genuine and certainly significant part of being involved in outreach is the involvement of the body that does the sending. The local body must have a desire to be involved in/with the work and share in the responsibility of getting it done.

> Anecdote: Cults and "isms" deny the Deity of Christ. Others simply distort the Word of God to suit their purpose. In a work place Bible Study, Christ was incorrectly referred to as "a" word instead of "the" Word. Since an entire doctrine of the Christian faith pivots on this understanding, it was important to correct the statement. The study leader challenged the individual, who responded, "Well, that is my understanding." The individual had an excellent standing within the company and if left unchallenged, the comment could have persuaded others present to doubt a specific reference in the Word of God. The study leader asked the individual if he would be willing to submit his statement to the scrutiny of the original text. He said, "No, I am comfortable with the instruction I have received from my Elder." To that the study leader responded, "Then we can at least agree that there is another opinion concerning the matter, and, that God has the last word." The individual openly agreed with that statement. May not have ended the debate, but it did not allow an "ism" representative to simply and unabashedly deny the Deity of Christ.

I worked with a good man who was caught-up in an "ism." He had been raised Baptist but somewhere down the road he became disillusioned and grabbed onto the feel-good ministry of a works based system of theology. Evidently there was no one in his life during that time to affirm the truth of Christ and he was swept-up by the religious dogma of an "ism." He and I often shared rides to and from work. It was a good time to talk about spiritual things. He would espouse some tenants of his understandings of the extra-biblical writings he had come to accept as truth and I would talk about some of the counter points expressed in the Bible. All of our discussions were friendly. He would always agree that the Bible is true as far as it goes, but he had newer, or at least more current, information from God through his Elder and the writings he had come to believe were more reliable than the Scriptures. That being the way things were, a more grave situation developed.

A mutual friend and long time work associate of both this good man and myself was kidnapped and brutally murdered. His wife and children were left without a husband and father. And, as serious as this was, it went further awry.

As the months passed, the wife and children of the work associate were ministered to by the good man and the "church" associated with the "ism." It appears there were no believers involved with the family through their local church. When this family needed help, the "good work" was done by the good man and his fellow good workers. The family's needs were met and they were absorbed into the "ism."

While I no longer question God as to why or how this could happen, I still question myself at times. If I had been more persuasive with the good man perhaps his commitment to the "ism" could have been broken. If I had been more sensitive to the special needs of the family perhaps their Christian faith would have sustained them and they would have found new hope in Christ instead of the "ism." It comes back to the local body of believers being committed to outreach.

Local Body Must Make Itself Available

As important as having the desire to be involved is, more important for the work of outreach is the fact that a local body must make itself available. There are many believers "on fire for God" who are involved with local bodies, but regretfully, some of these bodies cannot, will not, or have not, made themselves available for the work. Many are caught up in time monopolizing programs and overlook, even to the point of dismissing those who would be involved in outreach.

> Anecdote: A believer and member of a local denominational church became enthused about becoming involved in outreach and witnessing. After much prayer and soul searching he approached an Associate Pastor and requested a personal meeting with the leadership group to present his position. At the meeting he was congratulated for having come to an awareness of God's working in his life. But he was surprised when he asked the Associate Pastor what he could do in the church to help spread the enthusiasm for evangelism.

> The Associate Pastor informed him: The church had a full program in place for the next several quarters; that there was no provision in the schedule to accommodate any additional elements or obligate the facilities for any new activities; that the church was already involved in multiple projects; and that taking on any new responsibilities at that time would be inappropriate. As for a program to encourage outreach and witnessing, there just wasn't anyone available to take on that responsibility. Even though the member made himself available, there was no acceptance of him by the leadership group.

The enthusiastic believer was disappointed but he accepted the position as explained by the Associate Pastor and he returned to his regular place in the congregation. The "programs" went on as scheduled and the enthusiasm for outreach waned.

Witnessing, evangelizing and outreach should not be an over-consuming part of a local body. But, a local body should deliberately and with purpose, make itself available to grow the family of God wherever it is led by the Holy Spirit. Being open to that leading is a very important aspect of a local body of believers.

During an account written in the first century of the Christian era, the Apostle Peter was forceful in his message to the Nation of Israel, when they asked his counsel as to what they should do in response to hearing the truth about Christ. He told them, "'Repent and be baptized, every one of you, in the name of Jesus Christ for the forgiveness of your sins. And you will receive the gift of the Holy Spirit. The promise is for you and your children and for all who are far off—for all whom the Lord our God will call.' With many other words he warned them; and he pleaded with them, 'Save yourselves from this corrupt generation.' Those who accepted his message were baptized, and about three thousand were added to their number that day. They devoted themselves to the apostles' teaching and to the fellowship, to the breaking of bread and to prayer. Everyone was filled with awe, and many wonders and miraculous signs were done by the apostles. All the believers were together and had everything in common. Selling their possessions and goods, they gave to anyone as he had need. Every day they continued to meet together in the temple courts. They broke bread in their homes and ate together with glad and sincere hearts, praising God and enjoying the favor of all the people. And the Lord added to their number daily those who were being saved." [11]

After we accept Christ and His gift of salvation, we are to follow Him by: Being in fellowship with other believers, sharing what God has done in our lives, praying for one another, encouraging one another, and caring. Caring enough about those who have not heard to be available to get the Word out, and if not called ourselves, be there for those who are.

We are also to support those involved in the work of outreach. In Paul's second letter to the Corinthians, he challenged the believers there to support those who were doing the work. He ". . . thought it necessary to urge the brothers to visit you in advance and finish the arrangements for the generous gift you had promised. Then it will be ready as a generous gift, not as one grudgingly given." [12] Obviously this includes fiscal assistance, but it also means support in all other areas as well.

We need to exhort and encourage one another on a daily basis. We are all witnesses to those who have not yet received or heard the truth of Christ, let alone accepted the gift of salvation. All God is asking any believer is to be a conduit for the truth that lives within them. We need to be encouraged regularly so that we can feel the joy of sharing our faith. The local body has the responsibility of being available to do this. Not as a program, but a process where those who need exhorting and instruction can receive it as a matter of course; prayerfully and not as an exception. The writer to the Hebrews put it this way, ". . . encourage one another daily, as long as it is called today, so that none of you may be hardened by sin's deceitfulness." [13]

Work Must be Grounded in Local Body

God has touched us. Our lives have been changed and now we are to be contagious. Our love of God should be observable and be a genuine part of our every day life. That takes energy. And that requires an energy source. Most certainly God is our source, but where do we go to get our batteries recharged? Our place is to be with believers. "Let us hold unswervingly to the hope we profess, for He who promised is faithful. And let us consider how we may spur one another on toward love and good deeds. Let us not give up meeting together, as some are in the habit of doing, but let us encourage one another—and all the more as you see the Day approaching." [14] Where better to follow God's leading for our lives than in a local body of believers?

A local body of believers comes together in response to God's call on the lives of a few in God's family. Because it is local, this body of believers is positioned to grow in faith and represent God in getting the truth out to those who have not heard or who may have rejected God's plan of salvation. This position carries the responsibility of being true to the Word of God and, without compromise, having a good position in the community. The Apostle Peter made this charge in his first epistle when he wrote, "Live such good lives among the pagans that, though they accuse you of doing wrong, they may see your good deeds and glorify God on the day He visits us." [15]

Peter began his first epistle, "To God's elect, strangers in the world, scattered throughout Pontus, Galatia, Cappadocia, Asia and Bithynia, who have been chosen according to the foreknowledge of God the Father, through the sanctifying work of the Spirit, for obedience to Jesus Christ and sprinkling by His blood. Grace and peace be yours in abundance" [16] Obedience is part of the Great Commission.

Regardless of denominational interpretations or eschatological under-standings, being available to do God's work involves being part of a local body of believers. And, a large part of that commitment requires a desire of the local body of believers to be involved.

In Calm Answers for a Confused Church, Charles Swindoll relates that, ". . . in our Christian walk we learn best when we're not only told, but shown—when somebody pulls us from the church pews, seminar halls, and bookstores and disciples us one-on-one through the everyday disciplines of the Christian life.

That's how we become best equipped with the skills to live the good news of Jesus victoriously. And, consequently, how we are best able to spread the good news so that others will decide to follow Him too." [a]

Some years ago, while part of a Bible Fellowship Church in Garland, TX, I was part of an outreach group that regularly met for encouragement, instruction and visitations in the local community. The teams included lay-folks, seminary students and pastor teachers. Those with less experience were paired with those with evangelistic experience. Together we went into the neighborhoods around the church to share Christ and become more aware of needs in the community. Oftentimes we encountered situations that challenged even the most seasoned members of our teams. Afterwards we would meet with other teams at the church to discuss the results of our witnessing efforts. This was a very rewarding time for all of us. Not only did we learn about specific needs in the community, we also grew in our own faith-walk. We profited from each experience and learned first hand how God can take you into unusual circumstances and then sustain you through the process. It was truly a time when faith was tested and God's love was proven again and again.

"Lone Ranger" Evangelism is Not Required

You have probably seen, or perhaps been around someone who is "on fire" for a cause. Nothing wrong with enthusiasm. But, where is that person today? If that person is still effective for the "cause," it is a good bet that person was/is not acting alone. Paul may have been a maverick, but he was not a "lone ranger." He not only went on his journeys with others, he was also sent by a body of believers to whom he had become submissive. He was subordinate to Christ and submitted himself to that position. "Submit to one another out of reverence for Christ." [17] Submission is part of the evidence of our commitment. The church at Antioch provided the recommendation, ". . . where they had been committed to the grace of God for the work they had now completed." [18] There should always be a "we" in outreach. The world may see us as individuals, but even the Lone Ranger had Tonto. One with God is a majority for sure, and with this truth we can stand alone. But, we do not have to and should not be on our own. Especially in a witnessing or outreach environment. We may not agree with their message or their interpretations of Scripture, but when "they" stand at our door it is obvious they are there with a purpose and usually as a team. Our response is fairly predictable: No! Some of us may actually tell them: We're Christians, then quickly shut (slam) the door. This is called "opportunity lost." We can qualify our position and use these encounters to share the truth of Jesus, but only if we are prepared. Part of this preparedness comes from knowing we are not alone.

My home is a sanctuary. While we do worship in our home, it is not a worshiping center. It is a sanctuary for my family and me to be secure in our own environment. It is a place where I control who is allowed to enter and when they must leave. It is not a hiding place but "unknowns" and other uninvited visitors are usually turned away. However, as a Christian, I am mindful of God's Word where the writer of Hebrews tells us to ". . . not forget to entertain strangers, for by so doing some people have entertained angels without knowing it." [19] This is not a directive for us to set aside common sense or to abandon our personal responsibility of being aware of what is happening around us. As a young believer, I thought my response to this Word from God was to accept it as my personal ordination. So, when "they" came to my door I was eager to take "them" on and confront their misguided enthusiasm for a distorted understanding of spiritual development. One such encounter always gives me cause to pause.

I was home with my wife and children when the "knock" was heard at our door. I opened the door to find two smiling faces and a general question poised and ready. "Do you have a genuine understanding of eternity and where you will spend it? Do you know where your family will spend it?" And with hardly a breath, another barrage of question came rushing at me. I knew that I knew the truth but I became flustered and when I caught my own breath, I went straight at them. "Don't you folks know that what you are sharing is a lie from the depths of Hell? You have a distorted message filled with untruths and God will not hold you guiltless for leading people away from Christ."

My smugness was short lived. One of the visitors calmly and quietly responded with kind words and a sincere wish that I could know how wonderful it feels to be a Witness here on earth while waiting for God's timetable to run its course and those left on earth could serve Jehovah forever. There was no need for any type of argument. Everyone has a decision to make. I was offered materials to read and if I wished, they could arrange for one of their leaders to come to my home for a special time to study the Bible and explore the wonders of Jehovah's plan for all those who would accept and believe. Then, thanking me for taking time to greet them, they left.

Frustrated, flabbergasted and flat-footed, I stood there in disbelief. I knew the truth and was ready to take them on, but they were experienced and well-prepared for any contra-wise responses from me. I quickly realized I had gone at them with a feeling of superiority and when they quietly ignored my comments they seized the moment to say their spiel and moved on. I followed them down the walk and into the street where I attempted to bring them into a conversation about Jesus and His love for all of us. They were polite, but they kept moving away and their last words were piercing. "You can claim to be anything you wish, but Jehovah knows your heart and you can know Him too if you forsake the ways of a demon oriented religion and become a Witness."

I knew in my heart I was not prepared to seize the moment with these types of cult or ism related visitations, but I was absolutely certain I could tell them the truth when they came knocking. An opportunity had come and I was simply not prepared. That day and that situation may have been the catalyst that pointed me toward getting in touch with other believers whom I knew were involved in sharing Christ with representatives of counterfeit groups. With their help and encouragement I became more comfortable in my ability to share the truth of Christ when confronted by those who are sincerely representing a distorted view of God's Word or an outright hypocrisy.

Sometime later another team, representing the same misdirected group, came to my door attempting to present their distorted version of God's Word. This time I greeted them warmly and waited for them to complete their opening statements. Then, in a calm voice I asked them how long they had been committed to the beliefs they held. One said ten to eleven years and the other said about four years. Then, continuing in my calm manner, I asked them if in their visitations they had come upon folks who were strong in opposition to their message. Yes and sometimes were their answers. Then politely and calmly I informed them that my family and I are Christians. (Did you pick up on the politely and calmly?) I told them that if they had a few moments more I would share with them how they could know for certain where and with whom they would be in eternity. I interrupted their "stock spiel" answer and calmly told them there was no reason for them to continue their presentation.

I went further and also told them there was no need for us to argue on my door step. If they were open to hearing another point of view they could come inside and I would show them from God's Word the truth of how Jesus Christ is God; how He came to this world to demonstrate God's love for His creation; that He died for the sins of all mankind, yours and mine; and that on the third day, to prove His power over death, He arose and now represents all who believe to the Father. They did not come in and with nothing more to say, they thanked me for my time and left.

The point being, we are not alone and should not be "Lone Rangers" when it comes to witnessing and outreach. By simply getting with other believers I was able to get a better understanding on how to deal with those God puts in my path that need to hear the truth. By sharing my inability with those who were willing to share out of their own abilities, I was informed and encouraged with ways to respond to those who come our way with a wrong message.

A local body of believers should be involved and endorse any approved outreach ministry. Without the support and recommendation of a local body of believers, any program of witnessing is adrift. If we align ourselves with a local body of believers and submit to its leadership, "then we will no longer be infants, tossed back and forth by the waves, and blown here and there by every wind of teaching and by the cunning and craftiness of men in their deceitful scheming. Instead, speaking the truth in love, we will in all things grow up into Him who is the Head, that is, Christ. From Him the whole body, joined and held together by every supporting ligament, grows and builds itself up in love, as each part does its work." [20] Organizations can and do fill this role, but even they receive their support from believers.

Submission and accountability are important, but they are, or will be less effective without the support of a local body of believers. That support takes many forms. And prayer support is most important. No outreach ministry should be without a prayer covering at all times. It's a large part of the overall commitment. And, it's not as if God doesn't know what we are doing, or where we are doing it. We should be praying for one another. ". . . pray in the Spirit on all occasions with all kinds of prayers and requests. With this in mind, be alert and always keep on praying for all the saints." [21] Our brothers and sisters in the Lord should commit to prayer in behalf of those whom they endorse and support in ministry.

First Century Church / New Testament Church

While our status as an ambassador is a confirmed station, we also need to know we are part of something much larger than ourselves. Not unlike our own Ambassador to the United Nations, we have an identity within our family of believers, where there is a personal touch on our life. We also have an accountability factor associated with our position.

During the time of the First Century Church, Paul and Barnabas were ambassadors, along with Silas. Their journeys took them many places but they had a church home. "From Attalia they sailed back to Antioch, where they had been committed to the grace of God for the work they had now completed. On arriving there, they gathered the church together and reported all that God had done through them and how He had opened the door of faith to the Gentiles." [22] They were accountable to those who had sent them. The church at Antioch was their support group. The New Testament Church of today, represented by local bodies of believers, is our support group.

Our faith matures within a local body of believers. With Christ at the center, we feel empowered to do and be what God has called us to be. Paul understood this and told the believers in Rome, "You, however, are controlled not by the sinful nature but by the Spirit, if the Spirit of God lives in you. And if anyone does not have the Spirit of Christ, he does not belong to Christ." [23] As witnesses for the truth that lives within us, we are to operate in the power of the Holy Spirit.

Called, yes, but we are not free agents. Like Paul and Barnabas, when we go, we are under the authority of elders. ". . . So Paul and Barnabas were appointed, along with some other believers, to go up to Jerusalem . . ." [24] The local body of believers in Antioch approved the mission and sent Paul and Barnabas, along with the others, to be about the work of telling the truth.

Many are Called. Few Respond

Check this out. God has something He wants for/from every believer. Unity comes to mind, along with love and caring. Christ's ascension caused, or left some questions unanswered in the minds and hearts of many new believers. Paul answered them directly in his letter to the Ephesians: "It was He (Christ) who gave some to be apostles, some to be prophets, some to be evangelists, and some to be pastors and teachers." [25] It is good to notice from these words, that Paul said "some," not all. It is, however, up to us to address the "what it is" we are called to be in the family of faith. But we also need to notice that being a witness for the truth that lives within us was/is not excluded. That non-exclusion makes it very clear that we may or may not be called to a specific ministry, but in no way are we to shirk our responsibility of being a witness.

In Hand Me Another Brick, Charles Swindoll wrote about God's call on Nehemiah to re-build the wall around Jerusalem and how we should stay focused on the task. "Do you realize you can have your eyes in various directions in the Christian life? You can have your eyes glued on some other person. If you do, before long you will be disappointed or even disillusioned because that person will fail. Never set your eyes on some church staff member or church officer or another friend. That's the best way I know of crippling your walk. Instead, steady your focus on God." [(b)]

Christ is specific in His instructions. "But you will receive power when the Holy Spirit comes on you; and you will be my witnesses in Jerusalem, and in all Judea and Samaria, and to the ends of the earth." [26] He did not leave any doubt as to who would be the messengers. He wants us to start right where we were when the Holy Spirit came into our being and then branch out. (Turn on the water). Jerusalem could represent our neighborhood. Maybe the folks next door or across the street are lost and need someone to show them the way. Judea and Samaria could represent our community where we live and work. (Some of us commute). And, in our travels, wherever that might take us, even to the ends of the earth. Problem though. Few respond to the call. Did you? Do you know someone who has? Is it possible, or probable that our relationship with Christ is one of our best kept secrets?

> Anecdote: A commuter service provided assistance for many to live in a suburban location and pursue their occupational objectives in a nearby metropolitan area. One of the commuters, a Believer, put this time to use by simply making himself visible to those around him. A courteous "good morning" or "good afternoon," as the case may be, broke the ice. While every conversation did not result in a witnessing experience, on those occasions when it did the Believer, in a non-invasive manner, was faithful to his commission and in the process of conversation shared the truth of Christ. Over time friendships were established and many were led to make their own personal decisions about where they will spend eternity.

Whether we accept the assignment or not, we are still the messengers. In fact, we are the only plan God has ordained for getting the "Good News" out and about. Paul put it very succinctly to the family of believers at Corinth. "We are therefore Christ's ambassadors, as though God were making His appeal through us. We implore you on Christ's behalf: Be reconciled to God." [27] Even without a direct leading from the Lord, we are still ambassadors of Christ to the world in which we live. We can ignore our position and be less than what we are capable, i.e., a bad ambassador, or we can recognize our responsibility and become available to/for what Christ wants us to do/be, i.e., a good ambassador.

Fear and Confusion: Tools of the Devil

Talk with almost any person about sharing their faith and the floodgates open with a plethora of excuses as to what is keeping them from telling others the truth about salvation. The most common excuse is fear. Fear of what others may think, or fear of not being able to say the right thing. Perhaps the biggest fear associated with sharing is being considered a religious fanatic or worse, by those among whom we work or live. Certainly not a new thing in the Christian world. The Apostle Paul addressed this situation in his second letter to Timothy: "For God did not give us a spirit of timidity, but a spirit of power, of love and of self-discipline." [28] But, Ol' what's his name uses our natural fears to his benefit and generally speaking, we accept the more comfortable position of not being committed to any type or form of personal witness. We adopt a false attitude of contentment. After all it's not our job to get the Word out.

In an article titled *Fear of Witnessing* for the Institute for Christian Research, Henry Morris wrote, "More common than fear of physical persecution or personal harm, however, is fear of ridicule, or loss of prestige or position. Such fear is out of character for real Christians . . .

If we love the Lord and those for whom He died, we must learn to conquer our fear of men.

. . . How often do modern professional and business men—even theologians—compromise their stand for Christ and His inerrant Word because of fear of peer pressure in what should be their spheres of influence and testimony? May God give us the courage of Paul. 'I am not ashamed of the gospel of Christ,' he wrote, 'for it is the power of God unto salvation to every one that believeth'" (Romans 1:16).[c]

If you have never experienced fear in a witnessing situation, there is a good possibility you have never been in a witnessing situation.

Early on in my faith walk the experience of fear was real to the point that not witnessing was the result. Guilt was not in play. Just fear. I was a young para-professional working with educated professional superiors and associates. My social arena involved these types of people as well. When the urge to witness came upon me, it was easy to hide in my fear and just say nothing. More specific, not say anything that could brand me or cause anyone in my "associative process" to become uncomfortable with my presence.

Sam, a young missionary candidate at my church came into my personal area of Christian development. He could sense my uneasiness when it came to sharing Christ with others. He was an encourager and made a point of being an example before me for those times I would have an opportunity to witness.

One evening, while on a neighborhood excursion from our church, Sam and I came to a home where Christ was conspicuous by His absence. My fear was so prevalent Sam could easily have smelled it. He took the lead (otherwise we would not have gone up to the porch) and rang the bell. No answer, so a hard knock was Sam's next approach. The door opened and there stood a large man who was obviously irritated by our presence. "What the ✳ do you want?" (Obviously I wanted off the porch), but Sam quietly responded to the man that we were from the neighborhood church on the corner and we noticed his fence had been pushed over recently. If he wanted to repair it we were available to help. When the man asked why we would want to do something like that Sam was prepared with a non-threatening answer. "Neighbors helping neighbors is the Christian thing to do. Since Christ is our example, we want to follow Him. Could we help you repair your fence?" The answer was yes and some days later we did.

A week or so later I was at work when one of my professional associates came into the office on crutches. His leg was in a cast and his head was bandaged. Naturally everyone offered to help. More to the point, everyone wanted to know what happened. It was an accident for sure but the circumstances put most everyone ill at ease. The accident came as a result of alcohol abuse and my associate's part in the incident also included causing major injury to others who were involved. He was ashamed but he also had to work, even though being at the office was the last place he wanted to be. Our responsibilities required that we work in close proximity to one another. With his mobility severely encumbered, it was a normal if not the natural thing for me to be available to help with inner-office errands, break-time assistance, and just help-out in general. For all of which he was grateful. More importantly, I was there when the situation caught up with him emotionally.

He began asking the proverbial "why questions" and then as if by Divine Appointment, he came to me with an open question about my faith and how it was that when everyone else in the office seemed to be abandoning him, I was there for him. The fear thing just fell away and I was free to share. It was a natural transition from office chatter to chatter that mattered. I simply went to where Christ suggested that if there was one among us who had not fallen short and if so, then that person could cast aspersions with impunity. Since I was not that person, I could identify with certainty that I was in no place to judge. He needed to know that God is there for him and that if he wanted to affirm any aspect of personal forgiveness he should first come to an awareness of where he was spiritually. With that said, it was easy to set aside any component of fear and let my associate know about God's love for him and the provision He has made for his eternal future.

Not only is fear a major reason for not sharing our faith, confusion also plays a large part in our decision to let someone else do it. It's like when you are looking for an excuse, any excuse will do. We can even get confused from investigating what Scripture says about our responsibility. In a conversation with His disciples, following His resurrection, Christ told us, "Therefore go and make disciples of all nations, . . ." [29] This becomes confusing when we say He was talking to His disciples and that they were the ones to "go" and some how that leaves us out of the equation. Is it rational to assume that the evidentiary work done over the past 2,000 years was accomplished by those disciples and the few thousands of people with whom they could have managed to share the message of salvation? Most assuredly, others were involved.

In reality, this is the "Great Commission" from God. We are the ones to whom the Word is speaking today, and it is our responsibility to follow His instructions. By misapplying God's instructions we easily come to the conclusion that we are less than capable and that God will bring along someone else to get His message out to the lost.

Where are the Christians?

The noise is loud but the silence is deafening. Everything moves at light speed and we stand around watching and wanting more. More of what? No one seems to know what it is they want, and if they think they do, they don't know why. Everywhere you look you can see the results of what our communities have taken unto themselves. What Paul told the believers at Galatia is applicable today. "The acts of the sinful nature are obvious: Sexual immorality, impurity and debauchery, idolatry and witchcraft, hatred, discord, jealousy, fits of rage, selfish ambition, dissensions, factions and envy, drunkenness, orgies and the like. I warn you, as I did before, that those who live like this will not inherit the kingdom of God." [30]

> Anecdote: It is not your place to "judge" anyone, but
> it is your place to know better and act accordingly. We
> aren't even shocked anymore when we come in contact
> with smutty language, risqué behavior, and out-right
> promiscuity. These actions are so common place, we feel
> strange if we say anything about it. We'll be branded
> "goodie two-shoes" or something worse if we take a stand
> for righteousness. Can it be so easy, or maybe more accurate,
> why is it so easy for Christians to just look the other way?
> Probably because we are not receiving encouragement
> from, or being instructed by other believers.

How is it possible that in our country today, we have become so complacent about issues that matter. We don't give much, if any, thought to what's going on around us. Like the proverbial frog, we find ourselves becoming more and more acclimated to the increasing temperature of the water in the pot, not realizing, until it is too late, that we will be/have been consumed by the boiling water. We are afraid and ill-prepared to stand up for what we know to be true. We tolerate bad behavior by those around us because if we were to speak out, we would receive the ridicule of others. But, we will openly discuss topics that present little or no opportunity for us to be challenged in our faith. When we observe blatant contradictions to the fundamental tenants of our faith, we remain silent. Political correctness has replaced common sense when it comes to speaking up for what is true and correct. Christians find themselves in a dilemma at times because of the uncertainties associated with witnessing for Christ. It just becomes easier to look the other way or even ignore someone or something that could result in controversy.

Regularly, on what seems an ever increasing basis, highly respected members of our communities are caught in sexually compromising situations. Men and women of faith are none-the-less susceptible to the temptations of immorality. Christian leaders are confessing to what can only be considered debauchery. People we genuinely admire come forward regularly with their personal announcements of being involved with necromancers and the practice of witchcraft. Fits of rage are becoming commonplace in our institutions of higher learning and in the workplace. "Postal" has taken on an entirely different meaning in recent times. Students, or any others for that matter, who have not been taught self-respect or self-restraint in their upbringing, are involved with drunken brawls and orgies.

There are those in government, business and even in our churches, to whom trust has been placed who seem to be more concerned about the fantasy of their own unfulfilled promises. Their example is weak before our eyes and there does not appear to be any who are willing to stand against the negativisms being handed out by an ever increasing number of so-called leaders who claim to be in charge. Our nation is at war with what can only be described as militant, religion motivated, terrorist zealots. And, somehow Christians are to blame? Only if we sit by and do nothing.

Anecdote: A very popular public individual was asked about his position concerning abortion. The question was specific to the on-going debate between personal rights and the Word of God. As a professed Christian and self-proclaimed Biblical scholar, his answer was somewhat alarming. "If the law grants permission in this matter and Scripture condemns it, then Scripture is in error." That statement fell on the ears of all who heard it, but no one challenged it or even publically winced at the remark. An isolated media incident? Perhaps, but the media was there and no record has been discovered where anyone there was willing to, let alone actually did, stand up for the truth.

Where are the Christians when it comes to telling the truth and presenting a more positive counter point? Are we so inundated with all the noise that some of us have become numb? Even when we look we don't see. James, the earthly half-brother of Christ, wrote that "Anyone who listens to the Word but does not do what it says is like a man who looks at his face in a mirror and, after looking at himself, goes away and immediately forgets what he looked like." [31] It's as if we have been lulled to sleep by the deceiver.

In The Best of A. W. Tozer, concerning *How God Tells the Man Who Cares*, A. W. Tozer wrote about *The Vital Place of the Church*. "The church is found wherever the Holy Spirit has drawn together a few persons who trust Christ for their salvation, worship God in spirit and have no dealings with the world and the flesh. The members may by necessity be scattered over the surface of the earth and separated by distance and circumstance, but in every true member of the church is the homing instinct and the longing of the fold and the shepherd. Give a few real Christians half a chance and they will get together and organize and plan regular meetings for prayer and worship . . .

Such groups are cells in the Body of Christ, and each one is a true church, a real part of the greater church. It is in and through these cells that the Spirit does His work on the earth. Whoever scorns the local church scorns the Body of Christ." [d]

Hell is Promised to the Lost

Probably the strongest feeling associated with the writing of *God Saved Me* is the understanding that Hell is a real place reserved and promised by God for everyone who rejects the substitutionary death of the Lord Jesus Christ, as payment in full for the sins of all mankind. And everyone includes us as individuals and all those we love: Our wives, our husbands, our moms, our dads, our betrothed, our sons, our daughters, our sisters, our brothers, our grandparents, our grandchildren, our aunts and uncles, our nieces and nephews, our cousins, and our beloved friends and acquaintances. God has His law, His justice and His love. He has declared that it is His will that none of His created children come to the end of their earthly life and go to the White Throne Judgment because they would not accept the truth, believe in Jesus Christ and secure an eternal place in His Heaven. (cf. 2 Peter 3.9). By faith and for the asking, Heaven is available to all who believe. Conversely, for lack of faith, Hell awaits all who deny the gift of life in Jesus. God's promises are real. Salvation is real and, because He cannot look on sin, so is His promise of Hell for the lost.

Even though some have foolishly said they look forward to going there, no one truly wants to end up in Hell. And, no sane person would make plans to spend eternity in a lake of fire. The Word of God is specific about Hell and what it will be like for those who are sent there. The Apostle Paul, in his second letter to the believers at Thessalonica, described Hell in part when he wrote, ". . . the Lord Jesus is revealed from heaven in blazing fire with his powerful angels. He will punish those who do not know God and do not obey the gospel of our Lord Jesus. They will be punished with everlasting destruction and shut out from the presence of the Lord and from the majesty of his power." [32]

In <u>The Biblical Description of Hell</u>, Kathy A. Smith provided a comparison description of Hell as "A place of hopelessness and suffering—as a woman is about to give birth to a child, many go through painful labor that can last from a few minutes to a few days. But through this painful anguishing time, there is hope that when the child is born this terrible labor pain will subside. Just imagine if you can if that pain was multiplied many times over and you would never have hope of it ever going away forever? You would do anything to die to get rid of the pain, but it would always remain and continue forever and ever and ever. THIS IS HELL!" [e]

In his Gospel, Matthew wrote, ". . . the kingdom of heaven is like a net that was let down into the lake and caught all kinds of fish. When it was full, the fishermen pulled it up on the shore. Then they sat down and collected the good fish in baskets, but threw the bad away. This is how it will be at the end of the age. The angels will come and separate the wicked from the righteous and throw them into the fiery furnace, where there will be weeping and gnashing of teeth." [33]

The writer of Hebrews made it clear when he wrote, ". . . man is destined to die once, and after that to face judgment." [34] Without Christ, judgment is catastrophic. In his Revelation, concerning the Great White Throne Judgment, the Apostle John wrote, "Then I saw a great white throne and him who was seated on it. Earth and sky fled from his presence, and there was no place for them. And I saw the dead, great and small, standing before the throne, and books were opened. Another book was opened, which is the book of life. The dead were judged according to what they had done as recorded in the books. The sea gave up the dead that were in it, and death and Hades gave up the dead that were in them, and each person was judged according to what he had done. Then death and Hades were thrown into the lake of fire. The lake of fire is the second death.

If anyone's name was not found written in the book of life, he was thrown into the lake of fire." [35]

Our concern for the eternal security of those with whom we are close, as well as those whom our paths cross, is part of, if not the full measure of why outreach, witnessing and evangelism should be high on the list of things believers in the local church should be involved. Randy Alcorn summed it up in his book <u>Heaven</u>, where he wrote, "The reality of Hell should break our hearts and take us to our knees and to the doors of those without Christ." [(f)]

Statement of Concern

Look around your own particular station in life: Professional, domestic, academic, whatever. Do you notice anything that is as consistent as the fact that we are consistently less than what we should be? The Apostle Paul in his letter to the Romans, observed then what we can easily observe today: No one is righteous. "What shall we conclude then? Are we any better? Not at all! We have already made the charge that Jews and Gentiles alike are all under sin. As it is written: There is no one righteous, not even one; there is no one who understands, no one who seeks God. All have turned away, they have together become worthless; there is no one who does good, not even one." [36] Appears that mankind has turned to its own devices.

Could this be any more true than it is today? Permissiveness is everywhere. Observing debauchery is part of our daily lives. Television, movies, books, everything has become debauched. Our schools no longer teach right and wrong and our government condones immorality at every turn. A country founded on the principles of Christian faith, now denies Christ. Paul is right about this as well. "For although they knew God, they neither glorified Him as God nor gave thanks to Him, but their thinking became futile and their foolish hearts were darkened. Although claiming to be wise, they became fools." [37] Our imaginations have run amuck. Our scientist can clone animals and fowl, but they cannot make the elements that contribute to a blade of grass. Yet they come to us with their plans for a richer and better life, while the world crumbles all around them.

With man (humans) in charge, cultures decline. And, just as Dr. Francis Schaeffer warned, the ultimate end of humanism is always chaos. Tim LaHaye, expressed the following in his book The Battle for the Mind: "Simply defined, humanism is man's attempt to solve his problems independently of God. Since moral conditions have become worse and worse in direct proportion to humanism's influence, which has moved our country from a Biblically based society to an amoral, 'democratic' society during the past forty [50plus] years, one would think that humanism would realize the futility of their position. To the contrary, they treacherously refuse to face the reality of their failures, blaming them instead on traditional religion or ignorance or capitalism or religious superstitions." [g]

It has been said in many forms and by many people, "We must stand for something, or we will fall for anything." When we allow the truth of our faith in the Lord Jesus Christ to be trampled under-foot and ridiculed in our homes and in the market place, we are surrendering our God appointed and anointed authority to be pushed aside and replaced by dogmas and other anti-Christ thoughts and actions.

In The Best of A. W. Tozer, commenting on The Bible World is the Real World, A. W. Tozer is quoted, "We must have faith; and let us not apologize for it, for faith is an organ of knowledge and can tell us more about ultimate reality than all the findings of science. We are not opposed to science, but we recognize its proper limitations and refuse to stop where it is compelled to stop. The Bible tells of another world too fine for the instruments of scientific research to discover. By faith we engage that world and make it ours. It is accessible to us through the blood of the everlasting covenant. If we will believe we may even now enjoy the presence of God and the ministry of His heavenly messengers. Only unbelief can rob us of this royal privilege." [h] If we abandon our position with God we are compelled to live within the limited life sphere being demonstrated by non-Believers.

In A Nation Without a Conscience, authors Tim and Beverly LaHaye presented the following: ". . . the effects of secularism couldn't have happened without the help of a lot of people who stood by and allowed it to happen. Because of the absence of Christian votes and voices, a minority of people have gained control of our most influential agencies, among them education, the media, and the entertainment industry, and now have the power to determine who gets elected to the government." [i]

From sequestered positions within our own particular groups of friends and associates, we sit, hands folded, while our government as well as institutions of "higher learning" are engulfed by philosophies and activities that are at best in opposition to the principles of faith we espouse as Christians.

Jan Karel Van Baalen, addressing the topic of *Approaching Adherents of the Cults,* in his book, The Chaos of Cults, wrote, "Make no mistake: the cults as well as the sects . . . owe their rise, in part at least, to the shortcomings of the churches." [j]

Every aspect of life seems to be involved in or with something that keeps us from exposing false teachings and principles which are coming at us from all quarters. The news is always negative. Where is the "good news"?

Commitment to Each Other

Earlier, in the introduction, revival was mentioned as being something the community of believers might need to consider as part of the effort in bringing God's truth to a dying world. And if revival is to work, it must begin within ourselves and become contagious by involving others in the process. That requires commitment. Something each believer can do is to seek out another believer, or other believers, and get better acquainted. Like minds produce like hearts and like hearts are committed to action.

As you work through this process, you will soon become aware that the idea of being available to share God's truth is one of, if not the most dynamic part of your Christian walk. Others will notice your progress and become interested in what's going on. If your local body accepts the responsibility God has placed in its care, support and encouragement for you and others involved in sharing the truth will be a normal part of the ministry and outreach. You won't be drawing attention to yourself, but you will be allowing the love of Christ and the light of truth to shine. We are directed by God to do the work. We cannot simply say we are saved and expect any unsaved person to come to faith. James was truly inspired when he wrote: "In the same way, faith by itself, if it is not accompanied by action, is dead. But someone will say, 'You have faith; I have deeds.' Show me your faith without deeds, and I will show you my faith by what I do. You believe that there is one God. Good! Even the demons believe that—and shudder." [38]

We conclude then, outreach and evangelism are things all believers must embrace. And it begins and ends in the local church. Some are called to a specific ministry of outreach, but we are all called to be witnesses for the truth. If we don't tell the truth someone else will tell a lie, or at best, a distorted rendition of who Christ is and what He did. There is much to do, but the work, requisite for our salvation, has been "done." We just need to proclaim the truth about it.

Questions

Questions go hand in hand with witnessing. They come from within and without. We ask ourselves questions so that we can affirm our understandings and be prepared to accept the questions from those who, out of genuine interest, honest curiosity, and sometimes deceitfulness, ask about the truth that lives within us.

Some will use questions in attempts to distort our position and discredit what we say about the "good news" we have for them. If we claim Scripture as our proof, even that can be used against us. We must understand that Ol' what's his name knows Scripture pretty well. He can, and often does use Scripture to confuse an issue. Out of context for sure, but in that mode he can declare that the moon is made out of cheese. Foolish of course, but we must be prepared to set aside the nonsense, stick with the purpose at hand, sow the seed by telling the truth and God will oversee the harvest.

> Anecdote: A witnessing team at a community college
> involved in a discussion about how the Bible is relative
> to daily events, was rudely interrupted by one individual
> who challenged the authority of God's Word. This person
> had become convinced the Bible was the root cause of
> all problems confronting all people in the world. The
> comments were baseless, but none-the-less required a
> response, else the discussion time would be completely
> wasted. In a non-confrontational manner, the discussion
> leader asked the individual if he had actually read the
> Bible. He replied that he had. To which the discussion
> leader responded with, "What portions did you not

understand?" The individual replied, "It is all lies, written by puppets of the church to control the people." When asked who had told him that he replied, "A pastor." He had become convinced that the Bible was the cause of all the world's ills and he wasn't going to accept any of it. The discussion leader then asked the individual if he would be willing to spend some time away from the group and point out some of these errors. He agreed, and over the next few weeks and several one-on-one meetings, the individual was exposed to the truth and came to Christ. Had the discussion leader simply dismissed that individual he might still be lost.

As part of an outreach ministry of a small church in Texas, I was involved in an on-campus ministry at a local college. Part of that effort involved meeting students and faculty members on a one-on-one basis to share the truth of Christ in the social arena associated with academia. We always went in teams, but usually split-up to accommodate the one-on-one concept. And, as you might have expected, teachers and professors were the most difficult. These individuals are generally set in their ways, so when they are confronted with a question that requires a specific answer, they pretty much hide in their intellectual capacity.

During one of my encounters I asked a professor what he thought about the Bible being regulated to the mythology section of the library. The jest of his answer was that the Bible was a compilation of stories made up by writers who were neither scholars nor literary professionals and that it should be in the mythology section and not in the main stream along with other literary publications. When I asked if he had actually read it, he replied that he had in fact read some of it, and the parts he had read were confusing, so he didn't complete a total reading. My next statement was more confrontational. So you haven't read it, yet you believe the Bible should not be considered a literary product. He was a published author so I also asked if there was any support for his books being considered part of the literary main stream. He said his work was contemporary and not based on unfounded historical events. I then asked him if he would be open to an honest presentation of facts associated with substantive claims made by scholars in support of the Bible. He said he was but he didn't have much time to devote to such an activity. I told him I would be brief.

I cannot say that what I presented resulted in a completely changed mind or a changed person, but I do know that from that encounter a professor was exposed to a few Biblical truths. I was able to present irrefutable evidence for the historical significance of Scripture and demonstrate some of the fact data that confirms the authenticity of God's Word. Afterwards the professor gave his endorsement for our group to hold a regular discussion time during evening class times at the college. During these times we were able to direct individuals with whom we had introduced the topic of Christ in today's world to a discussion group that could address some of their more detailed questions.

My ability to confront anyone, let alone a college professor, about Christ and Christianity in general, is an out-growth of a local church's desire to be available to identify, train and support individuals who want to be part of outreach, witnessing and evangelism. This type of encouragement should be contagious within the Body of Christ everywhere.

You might take a few moments from your reading now and think about some of the questions you have, have had, or that you have heard from others where you work, or in other locales associated with your normal day to day activities. Jot them down for future reference. Give yourself the opportunity of thinking through the questions so that when you encounter them again you will be better prepared to address them. Paul shared some advice in this regard in his second letter to Timothy. "Keep reminding them of these things. Warn them before God against quarreling about words; it is of no value, and only ruins those who listen. Do your best to present yourself to God as one approved, a workman who does not need to be ashamed and who correctly handles the word of truth. Avoid godless chatter, because those who indulge in it will become more and more ungodly. Their teaching will spread like gangrene. Among them are . . . [others who have professed believing] . . . who have wandered away from the truth. They say that the resurrection has already taken place, and they destroy the faith of some. Nevertheless, God's solid foundation stands firm, sealed with this inscription: 'The Lord knows those who are His,' and, 'everyone who confesses the name of the Lord must turn away from wickedness.'" [39]

CHAPTER TWO

PRAYER, THE STRENGTH OF WITNESS

P rayer is a most genuine part of a believer's life. However, it is often ignored, or replaced with other activities within a local church or institution. We need to focus on our personal communication skills with the Lord and become receptors so that we may be better prepared to inter-face with Him at every opportunity.

Primary Principle

Evangelism travels on its knees or it does not travel at all. Without a prayer base, anyone attempting to participate in an outreach ministry, or as an individual witness, is ill-prepared at best. Prayer is the primary principle of evangelism. Prayer is our link to the "home office." No one should go or be sent anywhere as a representative without confirmation. Prayer puts our mind in touch with our heart and allows us to focus on the purpose. The workplace is a prime example.

Is there a boss anywhere that would send someone out to represent the company and not provide the representative with corporate support? And, conversely, is there someone who would go out to represent a company and not know that corporate support was available? Probably not, in both instances. Think about insurance agents. They approach as a single entity, but they are quick to share that they represent a larger force. It would be correct for us to believe they also had been given instructions along with some encouragement from the company. This example is applicable to most any line of work. Even a tent maker needs support. And, with witnessing, prayer is the main factor of support.

From his prison cell in Rome, Paul wrote to the believers in Colosse encouraging them to devote themselves to prayer, ". . . being watchful and thankful. And pray for us, too, that God may open a door for our message, so that we may proclaim the mystery of Christ, for which I am in chains. Pray that I may proclaim it clearly, as I should." [1] Paul counted on God to sustain him, but he relied on prayer for his strength of witness.

And, prayer is the vehicle we are to use when the local body of believers is involved in the ministry of outreach. As a "body" we have a responsibility to bathe the effort in prayer. Through the inspiration of the Holy Spirit, Paul told the believers in Ephesus that along with the helmet of salvation and the sword of the Spirit, which is the Word of God, that they should ". . . pray in the Spirit on all occasions with all kinds of prayers and requests. With this in mind, be alert and always keep on praying for all the saints" [2]

Remember that "Lone Ranger" thing mentioned earlier? It is obvious that Paul was connected to a body of believers. Through his example all of us should be plugged in to a body of believers who are on their knees before God in behalf of any who have accepted and are operating under a "call" to minister and share the truth. Whether you are part of an outreach group, a specific ministry, or simply allowing God to use you when and wherever He wishes, prayer is primary to the effort.

God's Released Power

Prayer is not and should never be considered an inconvenient obligation. Through prayer we can approach the Throne of Grace and place our concerns and petitions at the feet of the Lord. Then God can and will release His power as He deems appropriate. When we have humbled ourselves before Him and submitted our prayers to Him, we are then part of the process. James, the earthly brother of Christ, knew Him to be true and faithful. In his general epistle to believers, he wrote, ". . . the prayer of a righteous man is powerful and effective."[3] He had more to say, but these words tell us where the power is and how to access it. We pray and the result is "powerful and effective" because God said it.

God said it, I believe it and that settles it, is an often used saying in the family of God. It comes close to explaining what this prayer thing is all about. In actuality, God said it and that settles it! It is okay with Him if we believe it, but whether we do or not does not alter the fact that God is the ultimate power and authority in all things. Prayer, in concert with an appropriate attitude (a contrite heart), puts us in direct communication with the LORD of Lords and the KING of Kings. In Paul's letter to the Romans, he posed a question that puts the prayer : power equation into proper perspective. Paul asked the believers in Rome, "What, then shall we say . . . If God is for us, who can be against us?"[4] The answer is obvious and quick in its coming. Now comes the point where we get involved: Do we believe it?

Believe is an action verb. You cannot "believe" in something and not act on it. So, if we believe God is all powerful, that He will do what He says and that our position with Him is secure, we should act on our belief. A demonstration of this belief is prayer. Privately and in groups, prayer is an ominous part of our response to the Great Commission.

> Anecdote: A local body of believers met each Wednesday for a mid-week prayer and Bible study. During this time, they sent witnessing teams into the neighborhood and covered them in prayer while they were out. Later in the evening, the teams returned and reported what had transpired during their time in the community. Of particular interest to this family of believers was an ongoing vigil for a man with an utterly disgusting attitude toward God and anyone who dared talk with him about Salvation. On a particular Wednesday evening, a team

returned and with them was that person. He had accepted Christ as his personal Lord and Savior and had come to the church to proclaim his faith. God had done a marvelous thing in that man's life. Do you suppose the prayers of those believers had anything to do with it?

Only the power of God can cut through to the heart of an issue that is keeping someone from knowing Him and receiving Jesus Christ as their personal Lord and Savior. God releases that power in accordance with His will in response to the prayers and personal appeals from believers, and from the repentant heart of someone who is lost. R. A. Torrey, in his book <u>The Power of Prayer and the Prayer of Power</u>, wrote, "Prayer has as much power today, when men and women are themselves on praying ground and meeting the conditions of prevailing prayer, as it has ever had. God has not changed; and His ear is just as quick to hear the voice of real prayer, and His hand is just as long and strong to save, as it ever was. "Behold the Lord's hand is not shortened, that it cannot save: neither His ear heavy, that it cannot hear.' But, 'our iniquities' may 'have separated between us and our God, and our sins' may 'have hid His face from us, that He will not hear' (cf. Isaiah 59.1-2). Prayer is the key that unlocks all the storehouses of God's infinite grace and power. All that God is, and all that God has, is at the disposal of prayer. But we must use the key. *Prayer can do anything that God can do, and as God can do anything, prayer is omnipotent.* No one can stand against the man who knows how to pray and who meets all the conditions of prevailing prayer and who really prays. 'The Lord God Omnipotent' works for him and works through him.

. . . prayer will promote our personal piety, our individual holiness, our individual growth into the likeness of our Lord and Savior Jesus Christ as nothing else but the study of the Word of God; and these two things, prayer and the study of the Word of God, always go hand in hand, for there is no true prayer without the study of the Word of God, and there is no true study of the Word of God without prayer." [a]

Praying in the Spirit

All born again believers who have received the baptism of the Holy Spirit have access to and may be operative in the gift of tongues, or the ability to speak in a language unknown to themselves, but discernable or interpretable by others. On the Day of Pentecost, as recounted in the Book of Acts, "All of them were filled with the Holy Spirit and began to speak in other tongues [*languages*] as the Spirit enabled them." [5]

As to praying in the Spirit, Scripture presents three specific references: (1) The Apostle Paul, in his first letter to the Corinthians, wrote, "So what shall I do? I will pray with my spirit, but I will also pray with my mind; I will sing with my spirit, but I will also sing with my mind." [6] (2) In writing to the Ephesians he wrote, "And pray in the Spirit on all occasions with all kinds of prayers and requests . . ." [7] (3) Jude, the brother of James wrote, "But you, dear friends, build yourselves up in your most holy faith and pray in the Holy Spirit." [8] Praying in the Spirit does not refer to the words we are saying. Rather, it refers to how we are praying. Praying in the Spirit is praying according to the Holy Spirit's leading. It is praying for things for which the Spirit leads us to pray. Earlier in his first letter to the Corinthians, the Holy Spirit inspired Paul to write, ". . . but God has revealed it to us by his Spirit. The Spirit searches all things, even the deep things of God. For who among men knows the thoughts of a man except the man's spirit within him? In the same way no one knows the thoughts of God except the Spirit of God. We have not received the spirit of the world but the Spirit who is from God, that we may understand what God has freely given us. This is what we speak, not in words taught us by human wisdom but in words taught by the Spirit, expressing spiritual truths in spiritual words." [9]

Everything we receive from God is by faith. This includes salvation, the infilling of the Holy Spirit, and all His promises. This also includes praying in a heavenly language. When believers "pray in the Spirit" they find themselves praying at a new level, generally far above their usual capacity and beyond their typical understanding. They may also use words they do not fully understand. And, the Holy Spirit may reveal issues about which they have no prior knowledge or idea of what they should or would be praying.

Praying in the Spirit is a supernatural form of prayer. It is God-led prayer. It is the Holy Spirit leading you in prayer to places you have no idea you need to visit. It is God shaping your prayer. It is God edifying you, strengthening you and empowering you with dynamic strength and understanding. Allow God to lead you in prayer. Allow the Holy Spirit to fill your mind and heart and mouth with clear thoughts and the divine inspiration of God Himself and the mind of Christ. God is not the author of confusion, but understanding, clarity, peace, truth, goodness, faith, purity, light, decency, strength, meditation, and most of all love. (cf. Galatians 5.22-23).

The spirit of man only knows the things of man. The Holy Spirit, as God, knows all things of God and man. It is in the Spirit that we are to pray, because God knows us; knows us better than we can even know ourselves. It is the Holy Spirit that leads us into all truth, not our own life force or our own beliefs and vain imaginations. The Apostle John penned the words of Christ, who said, "But when he, the Spirit of truth, comes, he will guide you into all truth. He will not speak on his own; he will speak only what he hears, and he will tell you what is yet to come. He will bring glory to me by taking from what is mine and making it known to you. All that belongs to the Father is mine. That is why I said the Spirit will take from what is mine and make it known to you." [10]

The edifying aspects of or from praying in the Spirit is most usually reserved for those times when we are alone with God in our private place, often referred to as our prayer closet. Praying audibly in tongues is a special thing between a believer and the Holy Spirit. Since it is a private activity, we do not need someone with us to interpret. Praying privately in tongues involves a special relationship with the Holy Spirit whereby a believer can release personal thoughts and receive special insight from God that affects the individual believer's life and/or the lives of others as well.

Praying audibly in tongues in the presence of others carries the additional responsibility of conforming to the instructions provided in Scripture. We are to respond to the leading of the Holy Spirit and refrain from "speaking-out" in the assembly unless there is confirmation that the words spoken in tongues will be interpreted for the benefit of all who hear. In Paul's first letter to the Corinthians, he expressed an understanding of orderly worship with these words, "What then shall we say, brothers? When you come together, everyone has a hymn, or a word of instruction, a revelation, a tongue or an interpretation. All of these must be done for the strengthening of the church. If anyone speaks in a tongue, two—or at the most three—should speak, one at a time, and someone must interpret. If there is no interpreter, the speaker should keep quiet in the church and speak to himself and God." [11]

As believers we should eagerly seek the gift of speaking in tongues and be ready to receive it so that in our times of prayer, whether private or public, we may edify ourselves, receive knowledge through the Holy Spirit and glorify the Lord Jesus Christ.

For What Should We Pray?

It's been said that advice is usually someone else's opinion, considered or not, about something that does not concern them. An outside view of this prayer thing may appear to be an opinion by someone other than those involved and sound like advice. Not so. We are all involved. Some just less intense than others, but involved none-the-less.

Charles H. Spurgeon, in his sermon titled *True Prayer—True Power*, said, "To make prayer of any value, there should be definite objects for which to plead. My brethren, we often ramble in our prayers after this, that, and the other, and we get nothing because in each we do not really desire anything. We chatter about many subjects, but the soul does not concentrate itself upon any one object. Do you not sometimes fall on your knees without thinking beforehand what you mean to ask God for? You do so as a matter of habit, without any motion of your heart. You are like a man who should go to a shop and not know what articles he would procure. He may perhaps make a happy purchase when he is there, but certainly it is not a wise plan to adopt. And so the Christian in prayer may afterwards attain to a real desire, and get his end, but how much better would he speed if having prepared his soul by consideration and self-examination, he came to God for an object at which he was about to aim with real request." [b]

Since we are all involved, a natural question would be: For what should we pray? The answer is plural.

Luke had some thoughts about this and one item on his list was **laborers**. In his Gospel he wrote about the Lord's instructions to the seventy-two missionaries who went ahead of Christ as an "advance team" to all the places where He would be going. "He told them 'The harvest is plentiful, but the workers are few. Ask the Lord of the harvest, therefore, to send out workers into His harvest field.'" [12] Not only are we to pray for those involved in outreach, regardless of the level, we are also to pray for an increase in the number of laborers.

In his letter to the Colossians, Paul encouraged them to devote themselves to prayer, "And pray for us, too, that God may open a door for our message, so that we may proclaim the mystery of Christ, . . ." [13] Paul instructed the Colossians, and through them, instructs us to pray for **opportunities** to share the truth that lives within us.

> <u>Anecdote</u>: While on an overseas flight a conversation between two passengers began when one passenger observed the other reading the Bible. An inquiry was made to that person as to what "that" was all about. Without fanfare, that person simply shared a brief comment about how important the Word of God is to the world and how it focuses on the truth. The conversation was overheard by another passenger sitting in a seat immediately in front of them. That passenger was involved with an "ism" and wanted to share some of "its truths." On a plane at 35,000 feet, one could say there was a trapped audience for what was about to play out. The passenger with the Bible was courteous and allowed the "ismist" an opportunity to talk. When that person took a breath, the question was posed to the other passenger as to what he thought about those ism-based statements. He wasn't quite sure he understood any of it. The passenger with the Bible, again without fanfare, or any "holier than thou" attitude, posed another question to both of the other passengers: Isn't it plausible, as well as probable, that God, having made all this possible (gesturing to the plane and everything around them), wants to communicate with us. He caused His Word to be written and ultimately translated into almost every known language and has made it available to us so that we can reconcile the events occurring in the world with His perfect will for our lives. And, since all of this (gesturing to the Bible), cannot be understood or interpreted without God's assistance, we need His help. This Book comes with instructions. Specifically, that this Book requires

the interpretive assistance of the Holy Spirit, and it tells us how to get it. Would you be interested in having this knowledge revealed to you? At this point the "ismist" abandoned the conversation, but the other passenger said he would like to know. Using the Word of God, the other passenger was introduced to the truth. God had provided an opportunity and the Bible reading passenger was available. Coincidental? Not a chance.

From my position with a Dallas, TX based consulting firm, it became necessary that I make frequent and unscheduled trips to another city. A local commuter airline provided the transportation and on a regular basis I was "in the air" and part of a sequestered group of people for the duration of those flights. I prayed regularly for opportunities to share God's truth with others and in that regular situation those prayers were answered. Often those trips were made with an associate or a client. But usually I was alone and just on board as another passenger.

While every trip did not result in a sharing experience, more often than not, conversations moved away from trivial exchanges to more personal matters. Encouraged by prayer, mine and those of fellow believers at my church, I was empowered by the Holy Spirit on many occasions to focus discussions toward spiritual things.

God knows our hearts and is completely aware of the challenges associated with sharing the truth of Christ's supreme sacrifice and eternal security with other people. He used His influence on Doctor Luke and inspired him to write the *Acts of the Apostles*, which included a petition to God concerning the obstacles we will encounter in witnessing to those who do not yet believe in or accept the work done by Christ in their behalf. Part of the "Believers' Prayer" says, . . . "Lord, consider their threats and enable your servants to speak your Word with great boldness." [14] The Apostle Paul also had something to say about **boldness** in our witnessing. He asked the believers at Ephesus to, "Pray also for me, that whenever I open my mouth, words may be given me so that I will fearlessly make known the mystery of the Gospel, . . ." [15] Just imagine Ol' what's his name trembling because of our boldness.

Knowing what to say is almost as important as knowing when to say it. More important is speaking with **clarity**. We have all experienced conversations where we came away not knowing what an individual was really saying. When you know that you know that you know, it becomes part of your natural way of communicating. Paul asked the believers at Colosse to "Pray that I may proclaim it *(the mystery of Christ)* clearly, as I should." [16] Our prayers should include such a request. We will never have all the answers, but there should not be any confusion left hanging because of what we said. We just need to speak clearly. Leave the "big words" for more in-depth conversations at a later time. Cultivate the ability of knowing when to stop. It's part of earning the right to share more.

Praying for the **Gospel's good success** is also an important part of our prayer commitment. Paul asked the believers at Thessalonica to ". . . pray for us that the message of the Lord may spread rapidly and be honored, just as it was with you." [17] We have no less an obligation. We cannot expect our individual or collective efforts in sharing the truth to be successful, apart from involving ourselves in asking God to be involved in the process. Remember, we are the messengers. Some of those with whom we share the Gospel may reject it. But in God's perfect will, at that specific time, many may not.

The entirety of purpose for any outreach ministry is the opportunity for those who do not know the truth to hear it, and once believing, experience **Salvation**. The Israelites rejected the truth of God's provision for their eternal security and are now an example to the entire world as a "lost nation." They represent all who have and those who have not heard the truth of the Gospel. Paul was explicit when he addressed the believers in Rome, saying to them, "Brothers, my heart's desire and prayer to God for the Israelites is that they may be saved." [18] This is God's sincere wish for all mankind.

Further proof of this commitment of God is included in the instructions on worship written in Paul's first letter to Timothy. "I urge, then, first of all, that requests, *prayers*, intercession and thanksgiving be made for everyone—for kings and all those in authority, that we may live peaceful and quiet lives in all godliness and holiness. This is good, and pleases God our Savior, who wants all men to be saved and to come to a knowledge of the truth. For there is one God and one mediator between God and men, the man Christ Jesus, who gave Himself as a ransom for all men—the testimony given in its proper time. And for this purpose I was appointed a herald and an apostle—I am telling the truth, I am not lying—and a teacher of the true faith to the Gentiles." [19]

It is our privilege, in concert with our commitment, to request God to be a real and significant part of any outreach effort. Most assuredly, we can pray about anything, but in this category, we are being reminded to pray expressly and continually for:

- Laborers
  Those who will go into the harvest

- Opportunities
  Those special moments to share

- Boldness
  No fear of what comes from sharing

- Clarity
  Straight forward and clear presentations

- Gospel's good success
  Truth is not compromised

- Salvation
  Christ being accepted in the lives of others

How Should We Pray?

Knowing we should pray, and having some idea as for what we should pray, is a good start in our quest to involve our own spirits in regular communication with the Lord. Talking with God should be as natural as talking with our best friend. But, somehow many of us are so out of practice in our prayer life, we have trouble getting started. There are no "rules" associated with talking things over with God. However, there may be some value in having an outline, so to speak, in answer to the question: How should we pray? No better source can be recommended than God's printed Word to us. The following "process" is a ten-step outline that can assist our prayerful communication with the Lord.

- ***Praise***—David wrote to his director of music, "May the peoples praise you, O God; may all the peoples praise you." [20] God adores our praise and we should approach Him with an attitude of praise. Not only for who He is, but for what He has done in our lives, and for what He is and will continue doing.
- ***Thanksgiving***—One of the things that must be part of our "prayer tree" is thankfulness. God performed a miracle in our life when we were saved. All that we have, or ever will have, are by His grace and love for us. So when we are at prayer, we should have an attitude of thanksgiving, similar to that as written in a Psalm of Asaph: "Sacrifice thank offerings to God, fulfill your vows to the Most High." [21]

- *Confession*—We do not want to come to God with unconfessed sin in our life. We need to search our own hearts and regurgitate anything that might hinder our personal time with the Lord. James encouraged the followers of Christ to, ". . . confess your sins to each other and pray for each other . . ." [22]

- *Petition*—God is omniscient and therefore already knows the reason and purpose of our prayers. But, by asking we put ourselves in position to receive His answer. In his first general epistle, John tells us, "This is the confidence we have in approaching God: that if we ask anything according to His will, He hears us. And if we know that He hears us—whatever we ask—we know that we have what we asked of Him." [23] We must put our request before the Lord as our part.

- *Belief*—Doubt is the big "bugaboo" when it comes to praying. We know to whom we are praying. Most assuredly we know why we are praying. But, when it comes to believing, most of us have some work to do. Here too, we can look to scripture for God's thoughts on this concern. In his gospel, Matthew encouraged the believers with these words: "If you believe, you will receive whatever you ask for in prayer." [24] Belief is the key. We have to pray "believing."

- *Faith*—We came to Christ by faith. As believers we now must utilize that faith when communicating with our Lord. Concerning this issue, the writer to the Hebrews wrote, "Now faith is being sure of what we hope for and certain of what we do not see." [25] Just like "saving faith" praying faith requires us to trust God in the asking. If we ask in faith, believing that God will keep His promises, then we are in sync with our prayers.

- *Reliance*—If we are believers, and know by faith that God is always faithful toward us, then we, as grafted in members of God's forever family, must rely on God. The writer of 1

Chronicles penned, "The men of Israel were subdued on that occasion, and the men of Judah were victorious because they relied on the Lord, the God of their fathers." [26] Our prayers should be mindful of our reliance on the Lord.

- *Power*—We must not deny the truth, even though at times we become faint when confronted with the responsibility attached to being a person of faith. Paul, in writing to the Ephesians, made the followers of Christ understand that God wanted them to be full of the truth. "Now to Him who is able to do immeasurably more than all we ask or imagine, according to His power that is at work within us, to Him be glory in the church and in Christ Jesus throughout all generations, for ever and ever! Amen." [27] We are to claim His power with prayer.

- *Courage*—David was a man of courage. When he responded to the leading of the Lord he demonstrated it. In another Psalm for his director of music, he wrote, "Be strong and take heart, all you who hope in the Lord." [28] We should pray with courage.

- *Action*—The Corinthians were told by Paul, "Now finish the work, so that your eager willingness to do it may be matched by your completion of it, according to your means." [29] As God gives us utterance, He also gives us the ability to follow through. Prayer is a genuine opportunity to put our faith into action.

With these attributes as an outline, our time before the Lord should be more positive, conclusive and direct. It should also be understood that there is nothing formal or prerequisite associated with this prayer process. God welcomes our prayers no matter the method or process utilized to approach His Throne of Grace. The central focus is prayer. One-on-one time; just God and me, in behalf of our shared interest in reaching others with the truth.

When Should We Pray?

When to pray has been a foremost question associated with prayer. It can be different for each one, but the general idea is put forth in Scripture in four specific categories:

- *Always*—In the parable of the persistent widow ". . . Jesus told his disciples a parable to show them that they should always pray and not give up." [30] So then, we can adopt that understanding and "always" have a prayerful attitude in our life.

- *Without ceasing*—This is a difficult concept for anyone to grasp unless we understand that once we have launched a prayer thought we are to stay with it. Paul expressed this to the believers in Thessalonica with his encouragement that they should "pray continually;" [31] Obviously there is more to this, but the idea is to stick with it.

- *During the day*—While we go about our business and everyday activities, we should be conscious of our communications with God. Without question the music director in King David's temple was very busy and had much to do. David wrote in a Psalm to him, "Evening, morning and noon I cry out in distress, and He hears my voice." [32] David was declaring his dependence on being able to call out to God, and shared that with his director of music, and Scripture shares it with us.

- *Midnight*—In Doctor Luke's writings of the *Acts of the Apostles*, he wrote about Paul's time in Philippi, where he and those with him had been beaten and flogged and thrown into prison, and, "About midnight Paul and Silas were praying and singing hymns to God, and the other prisoners were listening to them." [33] It is not so much that the others were listening, God was, and Paul and Silas prayed. The results were dramatic. The time (midnight) was only significant to point out that God is available all the time.

For Whom Should We Pray?

We all have those who are special to us, and for whom we naturally pray. Witnessing, outreach and evangelism present additional opportunities and causes for prayer. We need to focus attentive prayers for *those who believe*. Jesus prayed before His Disciples, "My prayer is not for them alone. I pray also for those who will believe in me through their message," [34] The Disciples came to faith in Christ and led countless others to the Lord. Christ was praying for them. We should pray for them.

We are also to pray for each other. James, the brother of Christ, wrote in his prayer of faith, "Is any one of you in trouble? He should pray. Is anyone happy? Let him sing songs of praise. Is any one of you sick? He should call the elders of the church to pray over him and anoint him with oil in the name of the Lord. And the prayer offered in faith will make the sick person well; the Lord will raise him up. If he has sinned, he will be forgiven. Therefore confess your sins to each other and *pray for each other* so that you may be healed. The prayer of a righteous man is powerful and effective." [35]

One of Paul's requests to the believers at Thessalonica was "Brothers, pray for us." [36] He knew his road would be arduous and filled with trials. Those with whom we have entrusted with the responsibility of witnessing, outreach and evangelism should be sent under the cover of prayer. We should pray for *those who are going*.

What Should We Do at Our Local Church?

The primary message of *God Saved Me* is that outreach, witnessing and evangelism are part of the work being done, or not being done as the case may be, by the local church. There are multiple ministries involved with evangelism. Authors write "how to books" about it.

Evangelists travel from place to place sharing encouragement and instructions about it. Pulpits broadcast messages about it. Entire ministries have been developed for the expressed purpose of reaching the lost. But it is all based in the local body of believers. And, prayer is the strength of that effort.

Anecdote: The church was set. Excitement was running high. A well-known evangelist and his ministry team had come to town. The advance work had been done by volunteers and now it was time for the message. As anticipated, there was a full house. All the regulars and several new faces were in attendance. A spiritual fire had been ignited. The messages were great. The response was good. Decisions for Christ were made and many lives were changed.

The evangelist and his team completed their work and left. The church was reset to its usual configuration. Attendance returned to normal and the regulars again took their places. Some of the "new believers" were back as well. And, the fire went out.

In the excitement surrounding the event, no prayer vigil had been established. Enthusiasm waned. Complacency took its toll and the new believers were left to find their own way. Not the intent or purpose, but the lack-luster result was in direct relation to a limited, or possibly a lack of prayer being committed to the effort.

As a local body of believers, we should come together around the need for outreach and evangelism, and bathe the effort in prayer. In the process we should become committed to each other, and through prayer, we should honor those commitments. We should pray often and diligently for our pastors and teachers. We should pray consistently for our leaders. We should pray continually for those we have appointed and anointed to do the witnessing. We should cover them with prayer in their planning, in their coming in and in their going out. We should never send anyone anywhere without the cover of prayer. We should never allow the Devil to achieve victory over our prayers. And when, in the providence of God, we are privileged to lead someone to Christ, we should pray for them.

If we are not a praying church, we should become a praying church. A praying church is a "staying" church. The Apostle John recorded the words of Christ, where He said, "I am the true vine, and my Father is the gardener. He cuts off every branch in Me that bears no fruit, while every branch that does bear fruit He prunes so that it will be even more fruitful. You are already clean because of the word I have spoken to you. Remain in Me, and I will remain in you. No branch can bear fruit by itself; it must remain in the vine. Neither can you bear fruit unless you remain in Me. I am the vine; you are the branches. If a man remains in Me and I in him, he will bear much fruit; apart from Me you can do nothing. If anyone does not remain in Me, he is like a branch that is thrown away and withers; such branches are picked up, thrown into the fire and burned. *If you remain in Me and My words remain in you, ask whatever you wish, and it will be given you*. This is to My Father's glory, that you bear much fruit, showing yourselves to be My disciples." [37]

Merriam Webster defines Disciple as: One who accepts and assists in spreading the doctrines of another. A follower is defined as: One in the service of another. As believers, we are most definitely followers, and because we accept and want to be involved in spreading the "Good News," we are Disciples. We need to follow the instructions of our Lord and become "Praying Saints."

Where Do We (I) Fit in All of This?

More than just an interesting question, where do we (I) fit in all this, is a duality question. It deals with our relationship toward prayer and its place in outreach and evangelism on a collective *(we)* as well as on an individual *(I)* basis. We all belong to the family of God. Paul was specific in his teachings of the Romans. He told them, "The Spirit Himself testifies with our spirit that we are God's children. Now if we are children, then we are heirs—heirs of God and co-heirs with Christ, if indeed we share in His sufferings in order that we may also share in His glory." [38]

Since this a true statement, directly from God's Word, we can accept it and understand that we are in the fight together. Individually we must come to the awareness of our position in Christ, then, recognize that we must come together as believers around a common understanding: Prayer is a binding force for the local body of believers. Like fingers in a glove, we fit together in all this, through the vehicle of prayer.

We have responsibility toward one another. Christ makes the burden lighter, but we need to submit ourselves to each other, and prayer is a large part of the process. We are commanded to pray. God expects no less of us. We simply fit better in the overall scheme of things if we are in direct communication with the Lord.

J. Oswald Sanders, in his book, <u>Enjoying Intimacy with God</u>, wrote about how *Intimacy Involves Walking in the Spirit.* "The Holy Spirit plays a crucial role in sanctifying and maintaining us in fellowship with God. Scripture clearly teaches that our enjoyment of full salvation is dependent on our 'walking in the Spirit.'

It is one thing to step out into the Christian life, but quite another to maintain a consistent, intimate walk with God. The step must lengthen out into a walk, and that cannot be learned in ten easy lessons." [b]

So, the answer is prayer, and our *(my)* participation in it.

> <u>Anecdote</u>: They came from every quadrant of the church family. They had felt the tug on their hearts to be involved in prayer for themselves and others in the local body who wanted to respond to the nudging, or maybe more correctly, the urging of the Holy Spirit.
>
> A specific time was set on a specific day of each week for these believers to gather at the church for the expressed and only purpose of prayer. There was no message being brought. No social agenda in play. No time limit set. Prayer was the order of business and the Holy Spirit was in charge. Each prayer time began at the specified time, but ended only when a praying participant felt led by the Holy Spirit to bring the session to a close. On several occasions this commitment involved three—four hours.
>
> As they gathered, each one came in, found a quiet station and began to pray. Some came together by two's and three's. Some sat. Some stood. Most dropped to their knees. Prayers were sometimes audible, but generally very quiet or silent.
>
> On a regular basis hearts were touched. Broken spirits were repaired. Sins were confessed. Tears flowed, and as forgiveness filled the room, commitments to follow the leading of the Holy Spirit were openly confirmed.
>
> The process began with about eight participants. Grew to include more than thirty-five, and concluded after three

months with seventeen regenerated believers committing
to provide prayer cover for a witnessing team that would
take the "Good News" into the community.

I was one of the seventeen regenerated hearts that became committed to outreach and evangelism as part of the ministry of that local church. Week by week I could feel my own relationship with God and His Word draw me closer in my personal walk with Christ. When I was with those other committed believers the reward was special and evident. When I was involved in witnessing and sharing the Gospel, the reward was even greater. When I encountered opportunities to witness one-on-one, I was better prepared and certainly more capable. This confirmed in my own mind that this is the process Jesus had in mind when he commanded believers to go into all the world and make disciples.

What Can We (I) Do?

Just asking the question implies an answer. However, because it so personal, the question could, and most likely does, involve several levels of response. For starters, we can understand that prayer cannot be over simplified. True, it is a communicative function of our faith, but it is multi-faceted. Even so, the answer can be synthesized into three basic components: Commitment, communication and availability.

In response to a direct command from Christ, we can *make a prayer commitment*. When Paul wrote to the Thessalonians, he instructed them to ". . . encourage one another and build each other up, just as in fact you are doing, . . . respect those who work hard among you, who are over you in the Lord and who admonish you. Hold them in the highest regard in love because of their work. Live in peace with each other. And we urge you, brothers, warn those who are idle, encourage the timid, help the weak, be patient with everyone. Make sure that nobody pays back wrong for wrong, but always try to be kind to each other and to everyone else. Be joyful always; pray continually; give thanks in all circumstances, for this is God's will for you in Christ Jesus." [39] This commitment may take many forms and require different actions at different times, but a commitment to pray is prerequisite if we intend to establish dialog with our Heavenly Father.

As important as a commitment is to our prayer life, communication is the key. Communication suggests, at a minimum, at least two are involved, otherwise we would just be talking to ourselves. The real problem with this arrangement is you cannot trust the answers. Don't read anything into this. For certain, one with God is a majority, but we are not alone. There are many others around us who share similar concerns and with whom we can talk. We can *communicate with each other*. In Paul's letter to the Galatians he wrote, "Carry each other's burdens, and in this way you will fulfill the law of Christ. If anyone thinks he is something when he is nothing, he deceives himself. Each one should test his own actions. Then he can take pride in himself, without comparing himself to somebody else, for each one should carry his own load. Anyone who receives instruction in the Word must share all good things with his instructor." [40] When we communicate our prayer concerns with others we expose ourselves to the opportunities of ministering to those with whom we pray.

Availability can become a nemesis to our prayer life. Particularly in this day and age, where everything competes for our time. We must *make ourselves available*. Look at the word "Avail-able:" Used as an action verb or noun that suggests having meaning or purpose. Combined with able, meaning specifically, it can be done. Paul wrote to Titus and told him, "he must be hospitable, one who loves what is good, who is self-controlled, upright, holy and disciplined. He must hold firmly to the trustworthy message as it has been taught, so that he can encourage others by sound doctrine and refute those who oppose it." [41] We need to be available to do the work. In this light, prayer is part of the work to which we must commit.

What Will We (I) Do?

This is where the message stops suggesting and begins to meddle in your business. Re-read this section and get to the crux of the matter. If prayer is the strength of witness, it is not what will someone else do? It's what will I do? Once that becomes established, the "I" can become "we" and a ministry can grow. Or, at least, it can go.

The local body of believers must rise to the challenge. Collectively and individually, we are to **call on God** for His direction and assistance. James gave us the inside track when he wrote, "If any of you lacks wisdom, he should ask God, who gives generously to all without finding fault, and it will be given to him. But when he asks, he must believe and not doubt, because he who doubts is like a wave of the sea, blown and tossed by the wind." [42] God will give us His direction if we call on Him. When we don't know what we should pray, He will give us utterance. We just need to believe and have the right attitude about prayer.

Having made the call, we are to **wait on God**. David wrote, "Wait for the Lord; be strong and take heart and wait for the Lord." [43] The Lord's timing is perfect. Ours is flawed. While we are waiting we need to continue praying. His line isn't busy; it's a timing thing. Always remember: God may not be early, but He is never late. We need to be sure our line isn't busy, or worse, disconnected.

Being open to whatever it is that God may want you to do is definitely part of the process. You must also **be ready**. In Paul's second letter to the believers at Corinth, he congratulated them for their good attitude toward the work and told them," . . . . I am sending the brothers in order that our boasting about you in this matter should not prove hollow, but that you may be ready, as I said you would be." [44] Prayer keeps the line open. Then, when we know what God has for us, we will be ready.

Oswald Sanders also wrote about how *Intimacy Produces Spiritual Maturity*. Using the Apostle Paul's letter to the Ephesians for Scriptural continuity, Sanders wrote, "There are few more attractive sights than that of an increasingly intimate relationship developing between a father and son, as the latter matures into adulthood. A growing mutual appreciation and a sharing in increasing depth of thought and experience mark their communication. Each enjoys the other.

It is that kind of relationship that God desires to sustain with His children as they progress toward maturity. Just as the caring parent delights to observe a child developing an all-around maturity of character, so God rejoices to see in His children a growing likeness to His Son—the only perfectly mature Man. Such maturity opens the door to an ever-deepening intimacy, and, in turn, that intimacy makes possible and accelerates a greater maturity of spiritual life and character." [b]

The call "to" God may turn into a call "from" God. When that becomes a reality in your walk with the Lord, prayer will become a natural part of your being and doing whatever God requires. The process will need to include a "management program." Even when our instructions come directly form headquarters, we must remember that none of us are islands. We are to **become accountable** to our local body of believers. In his record of Paul's ministry, Doctor Luke wrote about Paul coming back to Antioch so that he might give an accounting. ". . . On arriving there, they gathered the church together and reported all that God had done through them and how

He had opened the door of faith to the Gentiles." [45] The process is variable, but accountability is absolutely necessary.

Questions

Paul told the believers at Corinth, "The Spirit searches all things, even the deep things of God. For who knows a person's thoughts except that person's own spirit within? In the same way no one knows the thoughts of God except the Spirit of God. We have not received the spirit of the world but the Spirit who is from God, that we may understand what God has freely given us." [46] We can and should take our questions to the Lord. As with the previous and subsequent chapters, questions are part of the process. These examples are certainly not inclusive or exclusive to the subject of evangelism and outreach, but they may be of assistance in focusing on the topic of prayer being the strength of witnessing. We should challenge our minds so we can be more prepared to pray ourselves through to the place God has called us.

- Am I a "praying saint?"
- Am I open to the concept of praying without ceasing?
- For whom do I regularly pray?
- Is there someone I know praying for me?
- Do I trust anyone well enough to become accountable?
- Do I have a particular or specific burden for outreach?
- Is my prayer commitment too large, or too small?
- If this "prayer thing" works, why isn't everyone doing it?
- What will my friends think about this "praying thing?"
- Am I growing in faith through this effort?
- Is my role as a witness being enhanced/encouraged with prayer?
- Am I closer to God through a commitment to prayer?
- Is my commitment to pray contagious with other believers?

As you continue your thoughts about prayer and its place in outreach, witnessing and evangelism, you could use this space to jot down some of your own questions.

-
-
-
-
-
-
-
-
-
-
-
-
-
-
-
-
-
-
-
-
-
-
-
-

Don't be intimidated by the number of dots

CHAPTER THREE

THE WORD IS A WITNESS

Don't Leave Home Without It

Won't Return Empty (Void)

Given to Us by God

Written for Our Benefit

Explore and Learn What God Says

The Word as a Weapon Against Demonic Spiritual Forces

Let the Word Speak, so You Can Speak to Others

The Word Used to Build-Up Spiritual Character

The Word Can and Will be Tested

Questions

The Word of God is a most powerful tool when it comes to witnessing. From it we get the facts we want to relay to those who have not heard the truth. We also get instruction and encouragement to continue sharing with those who have heard and rejected the truth it proclaims. The Word of God is the foundation of our faith. Without the Word we would be severely buffeted by the winds of darkness and come to ridicule for our efforts.

Don't Leave Home Without It

A catch phrase for a contemporary convenience card says "Don't leave home without it." Depending on the importance and reliability of the card, that statement may have particular meaning to particular people.

The Word of God is most certainly particular. And, with respect to being dependable and reliable, there is no equal. It is considered to be "the authority" when it comes to truth. The Word of God actually has the first and last word in the on-going debate between those who think they know and the absolute truth of/from God. In the Gospel of John, Christ made a pointed statement about the Word of God and its relationship with Him. Christ said, "If you remain in Me and My words remain in you, ask what you wish, and it will be given you." [1] In this context, the word "if" is a conditioned response. An affirmative answer will receive affirmative action. If "if" is no longer a consideration, then "remaining" in the Word is. It quite literally means to take up residence. We want to reside in the Word and have the Word reside in us. That way we can never go anywhere without it. And, the Word tells us that we are allowed to ask what we want because we are asking in God's will. God is then faithful because having asked in faith believing, He will do what we have asked. (cf. James 4.3).

It has been said that a little truth goes a long way. More truth will go even further. More truth is in the Word of God and should be where believers find it to share with each other and with those that are lost whom God brings our way.

After our salvation experience, our walk with the Lord is progressional. As the Word of God exposes us to more and more of what God is doing in our life, we begin to take larger steps. Our confidence in the Word grows and we become more aware of the choices made in the process. The Apostle John was specific, if not explicit, in his Gospel. He recorded the words of Christ, where He said, "You did not choose Me, but I chose you and appointed you to go and bear fruit—fruit that will last." [2] Notice who does the choosing. We have received the ordination of the Lord to be involved in the "telling and the going." Fruit bearers are examples, "good or bad," to those who would become involved in what we are doing. God is ready to meet us wherever we are and provide whatever we need to keep on keepin' on for Him.

Won't Return Empty (Void)

The Word originated with God. From His mouth to the hearts, mind and souls of those in whom He trusted to compile it. And it shall not return void. The Prophet Isaiah was most definitely a man of God and His true representative, now as well as during his time on the earth. As directed by God, he wrote about the effect the Word has and shared God's own opinion of its purpose. ". . . My Word that goes out from My mouth: It will not return to me empty, but will accomplish what I desire and achieve the purpose for which I sent it." [3] The Word shall accomplish what He sent it out to do. And its value to you will increase in the process.

Paul refers to the faith of Abraham in his letter to the Romans. He wrote, ". . . he (Abraham) did not waver through unbelief regarding the promise of God, but was strengthened in his faith and gave glory to God, being fully persuaded that God had power to do what He had promised." [4] God is all-powerful. There is absolutely nothing which is right, just or holy that He cannot do. And, He promised that His Word would go out and not come back empty. All we need do is let the Word do the talking. When you have an opportunity to share the truth that lives within you, start with the Word. You can say something like, "God says in His Word . . . ," then say what God says.

> Anecdote: A discussion ensued between two men during lunchtime at an office. One was experiencing a personal problem with his parents. They objected to some of his life choices and had requested him to not bring them, or the consequences they produced, into their home. He was having to deal with avoiding his parents or structuring his time with them in such a way as to not cause a situation. He did not want to be estranged from his parents, but he did not want to act differently than he was. He asked the other man if he had any suggestions as to how he might handle the situation.

> Along with being a co-worker, the other man was a friend. He did not wish to be a critic or a counselor in this matter and thought the better way to respond would be to simply allow God to speak directly to it. Without being flippant, he expressed an awareness of the situation and said, "I'm not sure I understand all I know about the circumstances but I do know that we should be respectful toward our parents. God says in His Word that we are to honor our mother and father. (cf. Ephesians 6.1-3) He went on to say that unless our parents are requesting us to violate God's will in our life, we should respect their wishes.

The door was left open to allow further discussion, but at the time of this discussion, the Word of God spoke directly to the question and the only option then was to accept or reject the instructions.

Everyone, believers and unbelievers alike, deal with life and the reality of it on a daily basis. Circumstances and situations are always changing and everyone has to work through their own issues to arrive at any level of understanding or coexistence. Talking it out or discussing our individual situation with others is oftentimes a way to confirm our position, or seek alternate opinions. For believers, this can become an opportunity to share the truth.

Common to our time is the concept of situational ethics. However there are some problems with this area of our lives today. Charles Ryrie spoke to this concern in his book You Mean the Bible Teaches That . . . with the following: "A basic problem with situational ethics is that it does not give proper place to a living God who has spoken and who acts in history concerning the affairs of men. This is not to say that those who hold these views do not have any kind of God in their system, but it is to insist that they have discarded the true God who has revealed Himself in the Bible and in historical time-space activities. Indeed, the God of the situationist is not the supernatural, transcendent Being revealed in the Scriptures." [a] Here again we are made aware of the fact it is God who speaks to us with His Word.

Given to Us by God

Some of the questions we have today about Scripture appear to be similar to those developed during the first century of the Christian era. Paul wrote to Timothy about the importance of God's Word and made it clear that, "All Scripture is God-breathed and is useful for teaching, rebuking, correcting and training in righteousness, . . ." [5] All means all and except in those instances where "man" has "tweaked" it, the Word of God is infallible. We need to know this because, one of the things God wants us to do with His Word is to instruct in righteousness.

Notice also the other purposes of Scripture: Understand doctrines of the Christian faith; to reprove a brother or sister; for correction, especially when you're dealing with someone who is bent in the wrong direction, or may be following a wrong leader.

> <u>Anecdote</u>: A self-proclaimed "apostle" was attempting to make a point about his particular understanding of God's Word. His position was quickly identified as being "off the mark" when he tried to explain that Adam had not actually defied, or gone against God's will, by partaking of the forbidden fruit. He presented the argument that Adam was obeying a "higher command" because God had instructed him to multiply and fill the earth. In her fallen condition, Eve could not be his partner and give birth to his children. It was necessary for him to follow her into transgression so he could be with her and follow the bigger command of God.

> The Word of God is specific and direct. Don't eat the forbidden fruit. They were beguiled. She ate. He ate. And, God disciplined them. There is no mention of a "higher command." This is man's attempt to distort the truth so as to accommodate a man doctrine that denies the inerrant Word of God.

With so many translations and versions of the original manuscripts, it can become easy to accept an interpretation of the Word as being in line with God's teaching and will for our lives, when in fact it is only man's idea of what God is saying to us through His Word. Peter, one of the true Apostles of Christ, had a few "God directed" words to say about the Word and how it is to be interpreted. "Above all, you must understand that no prophecy of Scripture came about by the prophet's own interpretation. For prophecy never had its origin in the will of man, but men spoke from God as they were carried along by the Holy Spirit." [6]

There is no private interpretation of God's Word. You cannot have one interpretation and the person with whom you are witnessing have another. This does not mean understanding, but interpretation. The prophecy came to holy men of God as directed by the Holy Spirit. We can possibly come to different conclusions, but we cannot have our own private interpretation.

It is absolutely essential that we grasp the understanding that God, in His omniscience, knows our hearts and the inner workings of our minds. Not only ours, but all of those who have existed before us and those who will follow us in this world. He caused His thoughts to be penned for our benefit. He inspired the Psalmist to write, "Let this be written for a future generation, that a people not yet created may praise the Lord." [7] A marvelous thing by a marvelous God.

God knew we would be coming along and need to know what He thought about certain things. His Word was written not just for the Jew at the time of the writing, but for future generations: All of us folks out here who need to hear from God.

Written for Our Benefit

Where is our hope? In Christ of course. How do we know? The Word of God tells us. In Paul's' letter to the Romans he said, ". . . everything that was written in the past was written to teach us, so that through endurance and the encouragement of the Scriptures we might have hope." [8] The Word of God is for everyone. Some reject it because they don't know the One behind the writing, or why He wrote it.

The Word of God is hope. In his first general epistle, the Apostle John wrote, "I write these things to you who believe in the name of the Son of God so that you may know that you have eternal life. This is the confidence we have in approaching God: That if we ask anything according to His will, He hears us." [9] This same Word of God is also hope even to those who do not believe.

Ever been at a hospital where someone was in real bad shape, maybe dying? Many of these people are unbelievers, but they are comforted by the Word of God. They become more peaceful when they hear the Word.

A co-worker of mine named Paul, had been ill for a fairly long period of time. He was certain he would die soon and even though he was not a believer he enjoyed talking about matters of faith with me and I often shared the truth of Christ with him. From his hospital bed he asked me about a situation written of where God used a donkey to straighten out a fella who was objecting to what he had been directed to do. I took his Bible, turned to the Book of Numbers (cf. Numbers 22.) and related the story as God had caused it to be written. Paul grasped the meaning of the story, and even though he thought a "talking donkey" was a bit absurd, he realized that Balaam had been tested, and when confronted with the truth from God, he redirected his actions and followed God's will.

I used this opportunity to share how important it is to be in a good relationship with God and to follow His instructions. Paul acknowledged his own unbelief and while he was not ready to accept Christ as his Lord and Savior at that moment, he was certain that God was in control. He did not challenge the Word of God when it came to the writer relating how God used a donkey to communicate with Balaam. What he thought was more to the point was Balaam understanding the donkey and actually talking to it. I shared how I would be glad to play the role of the donkey and tell him how he could know for certain that he was eternally secure with God.

As I had done previously on several occasions, I shared the Gospel with Paul and explained the way of salvation. I used the power of the Word to express the truth and quoted the Apostle Paul who wrote in his letter to the Romans, ". . . if you confess with your mouth, 'Jesus is Lord,' and believe in your heart that God raised Him from the dead, you will be saved. For it is with your heart that you believe and are justified, and it is with your mouth that you confess and are saved. As the Scripture says, 'Anyone who trusts in Him will never be put to shame.'" [10]

The truth was shared. Paul was at peace in his mind and acknowledged his understanding of the Word and that he knew what he must do on this side of physical death to be eternally secure in the Lord. He chose to not make a prayer of confession at the time but was genuinely appreciative of my having shared the truth with him. Soon afterwards Paul died. I could only be certain that the truth of Christ had been shared. What if I had not shared the truth with Paul?

God knows for certain whether salvation came to Paul or not. I know for certain that Paul had been given the truth. I had been faithful in the telling.

The Word of God is explicit: Salvation is of the Lord. The Word testifies of its own purpose: That we may know we have eternal life. Turn unbelievers on to this truth and watch them squirm. They have to deny God and His Word in order to maintain their sin controlled life. Give them the Word and if they believe, they get to share in the comfort, just like God planned.

Explore and Learn What God Says

As believers, we need to be ready to share the reason of our hope. We should get in the Word and get ready! Peter put it this way, "But in your hearts set apart Christ as Lord. Always be prepared to give an answer to everyone who asks you to give the reason for the hope that you have. But do this with gentleness and respect, . . ." [11] Paul told Timothy, "Do your best to present yourself to God as one approved, a workman who does not need to be ashamed and who correctly handles the Word of truth." [12]

Study. Spend time in God's Word. Rightly dividing the Word of truth. (It is part of this understanding thing). Look at whose approval we are courting. It pleases God for us to know His Word and use it to win souls for His forever kingdom. The Apostle John preserved some of Christ's encouragement when he wrote, "To the Jews who had believed him, Jesus said, 'If you hold to my teaching, you are really my disciples. Then you will know the truth, and the truth will set you free.'" [13]

Stay in the Word. Other materials may be fine, but stay in the Word. Read the other, but check it against the Word. Human authors tickle our ears and our emotions. God's Word simply tells it like it is and gives us the freedom to serve God on His terms, not some new program or idea that feels good for a moment. You can agree with what an article or book is saying without doing any research or study. Usually because we are reading something that agrees with what we think, or maybe we just appreciate who wrote it. We feel good about our agreeing. If we are in the Word though, we will know the truth and the truth will make us free.

The Word of God also addresses the issues of prophecy in our world. In his book The Bible and Tomorrow's News, Charles Ryrie wrote, "The study of prophecy gives poise and confidence in the face of confusion; it brings comfort in sorrow; it must not be neglected because one-fourth of the Bible was prophetic when written; it can be used to bring conviction and conversion to bewildered people; and it ought to bring cleansing and consistency to your life." [b]

Anecdote: Manuals are part of this world's culture. Most every product comes with a manual or set of instructions. Vehicles always come with a manual to help a new owner explore and know some of the specifics and to enable the owner to become more familiar with the vehicle. Some read it immediately. Others wait until there is some type of need or situation that forces them into the manual. And, regarding vehicles, except those used privately on farms and in industry, a license is required for the operator. This produces a demand for anther type of manual: The Regulatory Agency's Driving Handbook (Driving Manual). With this booklet we are able to know the rules of the road and the law of the land, so to speak that is used to enforce them.

Appliances and personal equipment usually come with manuals also. Some are detailed and complex, while others just provide general information. In any event, without a manual it is difficult to enjoy a product's application or full intent. Without a Driver's Handbook it would be very difficult to pass a written exam and obtain a valid operator's license to legally operate a vehicle. So you see manuals are very important. Without a manual it is difficult to properly assemble and then effectively use equipment and appliances, or capture the value we anticipate from a product.

God's Word is or should be a believer's manual. With it we have the proper and appropriate instructions as to how we are to operate our lives. Without God's Word, we are left adrift. No anchor and most certainly insufficient sails to catch enough wind to navigate in rough or calm waters.

In the Apostle Paul's first letter to the believers at Corinth, he told them about the importance of the Word. "For what I received I passed on to you as of first importance: That Christ died for our sins according to the Scriptures, that He was buried, that He was raised on the third day according to the Scriptures." [14] If you ever have someone ask why you believe so strongly in the Word, this is where you want to take them. This is "the Good News" of the Scriptures. This passage has it all. Christ did what only God could do for the redemption of His people. All according to the Word. Fact is, if you can start here when you're telling someone about Jesus, you can finish here too.

The Word as a Weapon Against Demonic Spiritual Forces

Adam and Eve had experience with the father of all demons. They certainly were not the last to be exposed to or succumb to the influence of an external force that gained access to their minds and produced a conflict with the truth that lived within them. Just as God's Word was available for them then, (cf. Genesis 2.17), it is available for all believers today. (cf. 2 Timothy 3.16). God's Word is truth. Satan's words are lies, often masquerading as truth. More so today than in any previous era, the forces of darkness and evil are affecting the lives of believers and non-believers in every populated area of the world.

God's Word is explicit. He wants us to withstand the powers thrust on us by the "evil horde" and resist the temptations they put in our path. We are to be aware not only of who we are but whose we are. From God's Word as recorded by the Apostle Peter, who wrote in his first epistle to Hebrew Christians, and through them to all believers, "Be self-controlled and alert. Your enemy the devil prowls around like a roaring lion looking for someone to devour." [15] And, consistent with God's provision for His own, His Word gives us encouragement and instruction as to how we are to fight-off these attacks from Ol' what's his name's army of deceivers. In his letter to the Ephesians, the Apostle Paul was inspired by the Holy Spirit to write, "Finally, be strong in the Lord and in his mighty power. Put on the full armor of God so that you can take your stand against the devil's schemes. For our struggle is not against flesh and blood, but against the rulers, against the authorities, against the powers of this dark world and against the spiritual forces of evil in the heavenly realms. Therefore put on the full armor of God, so that when the day of evil comes, you may be able to stand your ground, and after you have done everything, to stand. Stand firm then, with the belt of truth buckled around your waist, with the breastplate of righteousness in place, and with your feet fitted with the readiness that comes from the gospel of peace. In addition to all this, take up the shield of faith, with which you can extinguish all the flaming arrows of the evil one. Take the helmet of salvation and the sword of the Spirit, which is the word of God. And pray in the Spirit on all occasions with all kinds of prayers and requests. With this in mind, be alert and always keep on praying for all the saints." [16]

The Lord Jesus Christ himself was tempted by the same beguiling force that attacks us today. After His baptism in the *Jordan River*, Christ, in His physical body as a man, was led by the Holy Spirit into the desert where he fasted and prayed forty days, all the while being tempted by the Devil, who, at the end of forty days, when Jesus would have been the most vulnerable, attempted to persuade Him to deny God and use His power to provide himself sustenance. What did Jesus do? Again God's Word is brought to bear on the issue of spiritual combat. Christ affirms the power of God's Word by telling Ol' what's his name, "It is written: 'Man does not live on bread alone;' 'Worship the Lord your God and serve Him only;' 'Do not put the Lord your God to the test.'" [17]

Using this example from Scripture, believers today can access this same power from the Word of God and confront and defeat demonic spiritual forces wherever they are discovered. In <u>Secrets of a Prayer Warrior</u>, Derek Prince wrote, ". . . Paul lists the spiritual armor that the Christian soldier needs for spiritual conflict. The first five items of armor are all defensive: girding our waists with truth, putting on the breastplate of righteousness, seeing that our feet are shod with the preparation of the Gospel of peace, taking up the shield of faith and the helmet of salvation. These protect the believer. There is no weapon of offense, or attack, until we come to the sixth item, which is the sword of the Spirit, which is the Word of God.

Here is the great weapon of attack. If you do not use the Word of God, you may be able to protect yourself, but you will have nothing to attack Satan with. If you want to put Satan to flight, if you want to get him out of your way, out of your home, out of your family, out of your business, if you do not want to just tolerate him and hold him off, the weapon you must use is the weapon of attack—the sword of the Spirit, which is the Word of God." [c]

So, if the Word of God is powerful enough to attack Satan, it is most definitely powerful enough to go after his demonic emissaries. A young girl in Philippi had a demonic spirit of necromancy and a mocking spirit. She "mocked" Paul and Silas to the point Paul felt compelled to deal with her. In his inspired account of what Paul did, Dr. Luke wrote, "This girl followed Paul and the rest of us, shouting, 'These men are servants of the Most High God, who are telling you the way to be saved.' She kept this up for many days. Finally Paul became so troubled that he turned around and said to the spirit, 'In the name of Jesus Christ I command you to come out of her!' At that moment the spirit left her." [18] God's Word to us, through Dr.

Luke, from the Apostle Paul, provides the key to this power: In the name of Jesus Christ, . . . The Word of God instructs us to use the mighty name of Jesus and to claim the Blood of Christ in dealing with demonic spiritual forces.

> Anecdote: A dear sister in Christ had unwittingly come in contact with demonic spiritual forces associated with witchcraft, the occult and meditative processes. Some of these demons entered into this sister's body and systematically began causing all kinds of physical and mental anguish in her life. She, along with her family became very distraught about her condition. She committed herself to prayer and fasting, as did others around her, but the demonic spiritual forces had found a stronghold. The more she prayed the more severe the problems became.
>
> The situation was made known to a well-grounded and Word centered man of faith who was the leader of a home Bible study group. After visiting with the oppressed sister in Christ, this brother in Christ took a keen interest in gaining some insight as to what type of demonic spiritual forces there were that had invaded the sister's life. At an appointed time in the home of the brother in Christ, with other believers and family members present, and with stern resolve and protective prayers being offered to God for all, the oppressed sister was anointed with oil and the prayers of deliverance commenced.
>
> Claiming the power provided by the Holy Spirit and with the authority of Jesus Christ, the Word of God was spoken directly to each revealed demonic spiritual force indwelling the oppressed sister's body. One-by-one, each identified demonic spirit was compelled to leave this

sister's body. Some left more reluctantly than others but they left none-the-less. The difference appears to have been the direct application of God's Word to the situation. Praying was good. Praying and fasting better. But when God's Word was claimed against the demonic spiritual forces, these battles were won to the glory of God and by the power of His Word.

Using anything that works or helps is better than using nothing when building an arsenal to deal with demons. Attacking is better than submission and leading the attack with the Word of God is best.

Let the Word Speak, So You Can Speak To Others

The Word of God tells us of Moses and the people of Israel. It tells how God called Moses apart and gave him instructions for all the people. "When Moses went and told the people all the Lord's words and laws, they responded with one voice, 'Everything the Lord has said we will do.' Moses then wrote down everything the Lord had said." [19] Moses used God's Word to minister to the people. They agreed with God and accepted His Word. Then Moses wrote down what God had said. And for a time they were obedient. From just a casual reading of the Pentateuch we can easily come to the knowledge of what happened when the people of Israel became disobedient to the Word of God.

During his ministerial journeys, the Apostle Paul went to Berea. As recorded in the Acts of the Apostles, Doctor Luke wrote, "the Bereans were of more noble character than the Thessalonians, for they received the message with great eagerness and examined the Scriptures every day to see if what Paul said was true." [20] Would seem that the Bereans were a studious bunch of believers. At least more so than the Thessalonians. They were ready to receive the Word from

God through Paul and Silas and they were also prepared to search the Scriptures to see if they were being told the truth. (Only Old Testament Scriptures were available at that time).

When we hear from God's men today, are we to do any less than the Bereans? There are lots of people out there telling others about Jesus and what a wonderful experience it will be and is for those who know Him and seek to serve Him. Problem is though, some of the telling is not in line with the Word of God. We need to check it out.

> Anecdote: A well-known and genuinely respected evangelist was meeting with a group of believers in a local church. The message was about salvation and the work to be done in getting unbelievers to accept Christ. As the message progressed, the evangelist began inserting a few personal convictions and presented them as part of the requirements for coming to Christ and accepting Him as Lord and Savior.
>
> Growth after salvation is a normal part of the salvation experience. Adding anything to the prerequisite understanding of the grace of God and accepting the truth in faith, believing that Christ did the work, is contrary to the Word of God. The evangelist had allowed himself to accept a small amount of compromise and had adopted a few elements of tradition into the message.
>
> It may be a common experience for those who come to the Lord in faith to take on a new outlook toward the church and their responsibility to it. To require these new commitments to be evident before coming to faith, dose not fit with what the Word says about being saved. (cf. James 2.18). The Word of God says we are to work "out of, or from, our salvation" not to work out our position in Christ.

Tradition had crept into the evangelist's message and those to whom he was accountable had not "checked in with the Word" or they had become complacent with the work and the ministry.

The Word Used To Build-Up Spiritual Character

An individual coming to Christ, in response to the drawing power of the Holy Spirit, arrives with a commission to grow in faith. Acceptance and application are then the order of business for the new Christian. Once blind to the truth it is now possible to personally see and feel the special relationship a believer has with God the Father, God the Son, and God the Holy Spirit. This special relationship is developed around the Word of God, upon which we build-up our spiritual character. Scripture reflects this truth with the writing of Paul in his first letter to the believers in Thessalonica, "And we also thank God continually because, when you received the word of God, which you heard from us, you accepted it not as the word of men, but as it actually is, the word of God, which is at work in you who believe." [21] Notice that Paul said it is the Word of God which is at work in you. Not just laying on the coffee table or tucked neatly away on a bookshelf, but "in you."

Pre-Christian era prophets knew the Word of God. The apostles and early church disciples knew the Word of God. They drew from Its truth and made It part of their lives. Their spiritual character was developed around their knowledge of and understanding the Word of God. In difficult times their spiritual character sustained them. King David was far less than perfect, but he was a man after GOD's own heart who was chosen to replace Saul. He had spiritual character. (cf. 1 Samuel 13.14).

Daniel relied on God's truth from His Word and was miraculously saved from a horrible mauling and death in a den of lions. (cf. Daniel 6.16). Obadiah, in obedience to God's instruction and with his knowledge of God's Word, pronounced doom upon Edom. (cf. Obadiah 1.10). Esther was responsible for saving the Jewish people as a result of her understanding the commandments of God. (cf. Esther 3.20).

The Apostle Paul was most emphatically involved with the Word of God as written by the prophets. (cf. Galatians 1.14). His spiritual character was well defined and respected by those with and to whom he ministered. When the work of spreading God's Word increased the apostles chose men who demonstrated spiritual quality to assume some of the responsibility. (cf. Acts 6.3). Timothy developed spiritual character under Paul's mentoring and was entrusted with an on-going ministry in Ephesus. (cf. 1 Timothy 1.3-11).

Miriam was more than just a sister to Moses. She not only saved Moses from being drowned in the *Nile River*, she, with her brother Aaron, was also a leader of the nomadic Jews who had escaped from Egypt. (cf. Exodus 2.4-8 and 15.20).

As an evangelist, Philip used his knowledge of the Word of God to minister to an Ethiopian eunuch. Philip was familiar enough with Scripture that he could, just from hearing the Word being read aloud, know where it was written and the truth being represented therein. (cf. Acts 8.35). The Word of God was in him and he was willing and able to share it.

Without question, we can claim spiritual character as an attribute of our Lord and Savior, Jesus Christ. He lived among those with whom he ministered and provided the example we are to follow as we seek to walk in His ways. A significant part of His spiritual character was

His ability to bring the Word of God into a conversation and focus His teachings on/from the perspective that "it is written."

As believers, our spiritual character is dramatically reflected by our personal knowledge, dependence and application of the Word of God in our life. In <u>You Can Make It</u>, Tom Williams wrote, "I have learned that Christians need to not to be surprised or alarmed when God does not change our circumstance or remove our trial. His own dear Son walked in the valley all the way from the cradle to the cross. No wonder the Scripture says we have a High Priest who is touched with the feelings of our infirmities, One who faced temptations just like you and I face . . . yet, He did not yield to sin.

I am so thankful today that the Lord Jesus Christ is the Great Comforter who comforts our hearts and enables us to comfort them." [d]

We must never become complacent in our walk with the Lord. We must "stay in the Word of God" to build-up and maintain our own spiritual character, while we encourage the same amplitude in others.

Reinhard Bonnke and Billy Graham are modern-day prophets and evangelists who demonstrate strong spiritual character by accepting and following God's will for their lives to take the Word of God to the whole world. Because of their commitment to speak the truth about the Lord Jesus Christ and his personal provision for the salvation of all who will come to God by faith, millions have been saved. And as God allows, millions more will be positively impacted because of their spiritual character.

The Word Can and Will Be Tested

Christ's public ministry involved the better part of three years. During that time He talked primarily with His disciples, but there were many occasions when He spoke to the masses. Many times He was unknown to His audience. His words fell on deaf ears and suspicious minds. The Apostle John recorded one of Christ's personal testimonies . . . . "the Father who sent Me has Himself testified concerning Me. You have never heard His voice nor seen His form, nor does His Word dwell in you, for you do not believe the One He sent. You diligently study the Scriptures because you think that by them you possess eternal life. These are the Scriptures that testify about Me, . . ." [22]

The Jews with whom Christ was talking did not know Him. They were attempting to use the Scriptures to test Him. They were trying to trap Him. They were in the presence of the promised Messiah and would not believe, even though the Scriptures testified of Him.

There are a lot of people today who think they know something from what someone has told them personally, or in a book, that refutes what the Word of God says about faith and salvation. They argue from a position of ignorance, but you can't convince them of it. This is where the Word must stand on its own. God says it and that settles it. They need to believe it, but whether they do or not, truth is still truth. The Word of God is where we can go to and come from when we are telling someone about Jesus. If they want to argue, then they will have to argue with God. His Word is our authority. We know it is true. They only think what they believe about the Bible is true. We know the truth. If they don't accept what God says, they are rejecting God, not us. The Word of God can stand any test from any quarter as to its validity, historical significance, or relevance to current issues.

J. Vernon McGee addressed the question of Biblical reliability in Doctrine For Difficult Days with the following: "Now if you should ask me, 'McGee, how do you know for sure this is the Word of God? I need something I can get my teeth in, something that I can stand on as firm ground, and know it's God's Word.' Well, I can give you several proofs, but the greatest is *fulfilled* prophecy. Hundreds of prophecies were fulfilled concerning Jesus at His first coming, *literally fulfilled*! Twenty-eight of them were fulfilled while he was hanging on the cross. When He was ready to die, as you remember, He said, 'I thirst.' They gave Him vinegar to drink, which fulfilled the last (the twenty-eighth) prophecy, then He expired." [c]

Christ Himself told His disciples, and through them He tells us the truth about God's Word. "He said to them, 'This is what I told you while I was still with you: Everything must be fulfilled that is written about Me in the Law of Moses, the Prophets and the Psalms.' Then He opened their minds so they could understand the Scriptures. He told them, 'This is what is written: The Christ will suffer and rise from the dead on the third day, and repentance and forgiveness of sins will be preached in His name to all nations, beginning at Jerusalem. You are witnesses of these things.'" [23]

This is like having the answers in the back of the book. Christ tells His disciples and us as well, through the revelation of Scripture being written and passed down. He opened their minds so they could understand. Our minds are opened through our relationship with the Holy Spirit that we received when we were saved. That same Holy Spirit that instructed the disciples, instructs us. All we need do is take the Word and apply it.

When we use the Word as a witness, we are using the sword of the Lord to battle those who would distort the truth and attempt to change what God has said must be. Every cult, occult or ism representative that comes our way must argue against what God says in His Word and prevail before their diatribe can be of or have any effect.

If we are presented a question or situation that we can't handle, the Word can. We need only to defer our thoughts and response to the Word. It may require us to say we don't know, but God does. If they really want to know, they will be willing for us to check it out and get back to them.

Questions

When the Word of God is your authority, rest assured many of those to whom you may witness will challenge your position. You will not have all the answers, but you will have the truth. The following are a few questions you may encounter in an outreach environment:

What makes the Bible so unique?

In many ways the Bible is a most unusual Book. For instance, it has a dual authorship. In other words, God is the Author of the Bible, and in another sense man is the author of the Bible. Actually, the Bible was written by about forty authors over a period of approximately fifteen hundred years. Some of these men never even heard of the others, and there was no collusion among the forty. Two or three of them could have gotten together, but the others could not have known each other. And yet they have presented a Book that has the most marvelous continuity of any book that has ever been written. Also, it is without error. Each author expressed his own feelings in his own generation. Each had his limitations, and made his mistakes—poor old Moses made mistakes, but when he was writing the Pentateuch, somehow or other no mistakes got in there. You see, it is a human Book and yet it is a God-Book. [d]

What about all those numbers in Scripture?

When looked at very closely, a mathematical mind will find that there is something infinitely intelligent behind the Word of God. Something (or someone) so intelligent, that the origin of the Bible could never be attributed to mere man. It must be inspired by God! [e]

A number which comes often to my mind is *666*. As the Apostle John wrote in his Revelation, "This calls for wisdom. If anyone has insight, let him calculate the number of the beast, for it is man's number. His number is 666." [24] No obsession is involved here, just the general reminder of how God allows specific circumstances and situations to occur in our lives. At a time when I was running ahead of God in managing the fiscal affairs of my life, I stepped outside the boundary of prudent decision making due to a personal want.

We needed a second car and I justified the need in my own mind. A used VW caught my eye and the price was almost reasonable. Reasonable because I wanted it and it was to be a special gift for my wife. I actually drove it and made a commitment with the owner to buy it. Then I figured a way to get it: With the required amount of money in hand I went to the owner and made arrangements to take delivery of the cute little red VW.

It was raining the evening I went to pick up the VW. Not a big rain, but enough to roll-up the windows if you were in a car. I noticed the windows were down on the VW. I checked inside. Not wet enough to dampen my enthusiasm for buying the car. I completed the paperwork and took the keys to the cute little red VW. On my way home I noticed a strong gasoline smell in the car. Our house was close by so I wasn't in the car very long. It was raining so I delayed the "tooling around ride" until the next day. Next day came and the gasoline smell had worsened.

The recounting of this inappropriate decision and actions taken in its support, does not improve with the telling. The gasoline odor was a result of a faulty fuel supply line. Compounding that problem was a failing fuel pump. More investigation discovered a bad carburetor and fuel filter. A few miles down the road the brakes went spongy. On the way back home, a tie-rod gave up. Barely drivable, I "limped" the car home. As the proud owner of that cute little red VW, I was not too impressed with myself. And, as if by Divine Direction, my eyes fell on the odometer which glaringly displayed the number 00**666**. Moral: Wait on God. Of course there is also the genuine understanding that you get what you pay for and you usually get what you deserve. And compounding the negative side of the situation is the fact that even though I learned from it, I did not honor God in the process. I could have, probably should have, used the cute little red VW as a good excuse to approach the guy who sold it to me and share a little of God's love. Maybe it is better that I didn't. As I recall I was not really thinking lovely thoughts at the time.

Do archaeological finds support or contradict the Bible?

<u>Manuscript (mss) Evidence</u>—. . . no other ancient book's text is questioned or maligned like that of the Bible. For instance, Aristotle's *Ode to Poetics* was written between 384-322BC. Our earliest copy of this work dates 1,100 AD, and we find there are only 49 extant manuscripts. Note that the gap between the original writing and the earliest copy is 1,400 years. A second example is Plato's *Tetralogies*, written 427-347 BC. Our earliest copy is 900 AD, and there are only 7 extant manuscripts to study. The gap between the original and the earliest copy is 1,200 years. What about the New Testament? Jesus was crucified in 30 AD. The New Testament was written between 48 and 95 AD. The oldest mss date to the last quarter of the first century, and the second oldest 125 AD. This gives us a narrow gap of 35 to 40 years from the originals written by the apostles. From the early

centuries, we have some 5,300 Greek mss of the New Testament. Altogether, including Syriac, Latin, Coptic and Aramaic, we have a whopping total of 24,633 texts of the ancient New Testament to confirm the wording of the New Testament scriptures. So the bottom line is, there was no great time period between the events of the New Testament and the New Testament writings. Nor is there a great lapse of time between the original writings and the oldest copies. This means that with the great body of mss evidence, it can also be proved, beyond a doubt, that the New Testament says exactly the same things today as it originally did nearly 2,000 years ago. [f]

Who determined what writings are in the Bible?

Norman Geisler, in The Canonicity of the Bible addressed this reoccurring question. His answer is, "Canonicity (Fr. *canon*, rule or norm) refers to the normative or authoritative books inspired by God for inclusion in Holy Scripture. Canonicity is determined by God. It is not the antiquity, authenticity, or religious community that makes a book canonical or authoritative. A book is valuable because it is canonical, and not canonical because it is or was considered valuable. Its authority is *established* by God and merely *discovered* by God's people." [g]

Is the Bible really God's voice? Is it True?

. . . we need to understand this book qualifies as our final authority. "Your word is truth,"[25] Jesus said as He prayed to the Father. Truth, real truth, truth you can rely on, truth that will never shrivel up or turn sour, truth that will never backfire or mislead, that's the truth in the Bible. That is what the Bible is about. That is why the Bible provides us with *the* constant and *the* needed support.

Think of it this way: God's Book is, as it were, God's voice. If our Lord were to make Himself visible and return to earth and speak His message, it would be in keeping with the Bible. His message of truth would tie in exactly with what you see in Scripture—His opinion, His counsel, His commands, His desires, His warnings, His very heart, His very mind. When you rely on God's voice—His very message—you have a sure foundation; you have truth that can be trusted; you have power that imparts new life and releases grace by which you can grow in faith and commitment. [h]

What about those "extra-Biblical" writings?

The word Apocrypha simply meant "hidden" and might have either referred to those books which had been hidden from the public or simply unknown by the public. The Protestant Church generally designates this title upon the Old Testament writings: 1 Esdras, 2 Esdras, Tobit, Judith, the last six chapters of Esther, the Wisdom of Solomon, the Ecclesiasticus, Baruch, the Song of the Three Holy Children, the Prayer of Azarias, Susanna, Bel and the Dragon, Prayer of Manasses, 1 Maccabees, and 2 Maccabees. During the days when copies of such writings were extremely limited and scarce, it would be quite easy for some writings to remain hidden from or unknown to the general public. Religious authorities might have merely chosen to hide from the public that which was considered as unprofitable for their own purpose, or perhaps contradicted the doctrines that they themselves had taught. We need only to look as far as our own denominations to witness a similar Christianized type of censorship. The evidence is overwhelming. Man will exalt one doctrine while suppressing another. It matters little which of these doctrines is true and which is false. It is man's opinion and man's doctrine which is exalted. Any doctrine which might jeopardize or contradict the denominations favored doctrine or belief must be outwardly suppressed for the sake of the denomination itself. There is usually no unction of God's Spirit which causes man to suppress these but man's own personal opinion. Usually there is no divine revelation, or for that matter no logical reasoning employed, except that the favored doctrine has always been favored among the particular religious sect. Do we think that the religious leaders before us were any different? [i]

Don't contemporary scholars prove the Biblical account of history to be false?

Josh McDowell in <u>More Evidence That Demands a Verdict</u> wrote, ". . . it often seems that a theory is accepted because of its place in a textbook and its continued repetition and recognition. Often repetition is a foible of scholarship. One scholar notes: 'Another common and natural phenomenon is the repetition of hypotheses once proposed.' As in other fields, so in Bible study, what begins as a very tentative guess becomes by repetition an assumed fact and represents 'the consensus of scholarly opinion.' *This* should be a warning, not only to the radical critic, but to the conservative critic as well." [j]

He also wrote, "Instead of starting Biblical studies with the presupposition that the Old Testament has error throughout, many contradictions, historical inaccuracies, and gross textural errors, the proper study should include a meticulous examination of the Hebrew text in light of modern archaeology and the knowledge existing of cultures of the ancient Near East in the third millennium B.C." [k]

What about Theistic Evolution?

What about it? Is that where you accept God as the creator of an initial life form, like the amoeba and the rest of creation is left to natural evolution? ". . . I do not think that you can logically believe in theistic evolution. You're either going to accept the Bible account or you're going to reject the Bible account. I can understand how an unbeliever can reject the Bible account, but I cannot understand how a so-called Bible believer can say, 'I'm a theistic evolutionist.' It's impossible. You either believe the Bible or you don't believe the Bible, and these two views are certainly in conflict. This idea today that you can reconcile them—well, it's a sad thing. [l]

What about Biblical eggheads?

If the question is meant toward those who know Biblical teachings but do not have a personal or Spiritual relationship with God, then perhaps A. W. Tozer's comment in *Bible Taught or Spirit Taught* will assist. "The great need of the hour among persons spiritually hungry is twofold: First, to know the Scriptures, apart from which no saving truth will be vouchsafed by our Lord; the second, to be enlightened by the Spirit, apart from whom the Scriptures will not be understood." [m]

Certainly not "all" the questions you might encounter, but these give you an idea of how to respond when they are presented. Just remember, the Word can and will speak for itself. We just need to be in it so that we can effectively share it and defend it when necessary.

CHAPTER FOUR

FEAR AND GUILT:
SATAN'S CONVENIENT PLOY

What Did He Say to Eve?

What Does That Make Him?

What Did Adam And Eve Do?

Then What Did They Do?

Why?

Where Did That Leave Us?

What Did God Do?

Can We Identify with Adam And Eve?

What Are Some "Current Day Lies" From Satan?

God Didn't Give Us a Spirit of Fear

I Didn't Witness When I Should Have, Now I . . .

Claim the Victory and Press On

Where Does God Say "We" Save Anyone?

Ol' What's His Name Will Do Anything

Questions

ausing, or giving us concerns about our ability to share the truth with others is nothing more than a convenient ploy of Satan. He will use anything and everything he can to confuse us and make witnessing as uncomfortable an experience as possible. Fear and guilt are his usual traits. If he can instill enough fear or doubt into our outreach activities, he can sit back and watch us go from being excited about our position with Christ to feeling guilty because we "failed" in our attempt at spreading the "good news." This is nothing new. Satan has been around for a long time. He goes all the way back to Adam and Eve in the Garden of Eden. "Ol' what's his name" is more than a trouble maker. He is a wreaker of havoc. Scripture shows him at the heart of every bad circumstance that befell the Nation of Israel and the emerging Christian believers. He set the stage for all of us to be in need of salvation.

What Did He Say To Eve?

In the form of a serpent, Lucifer, the very angel God cast out of heaven because of his attitude and actions against God, beguiled Eve in the Garden of Eden. God had made it completely clear to Adam and Eve that they were not to eat of the fruit of the tree in the midst of the Garden, lest they die. There is much to be said about the situation in which Adam and Eve found themselves. But, the specifics are crystal clear.

Moses recapped the situation when he wrote the Book of Beginnings under the power of the Holy Spirit. "Now the serpent was more crafty than any of the wild animals the Lord God had made. He said to the woman, 'Did God really say, You must not eat from any tree in the garden?' The woman said to the serpent, 'We may eat fruit from the trees in the garden, but God did say, You must not eat fruit from the tree that is in the middle of the garden, and you must not touch it, or you will die.' 'You will not surely die,' the serpent said to the woman. 'For God knows that when you eat of it your eyes will be opened, and you will be like God, knowing good and evil.'" [1]

> Anecdote: A brief comment about the origin of sin was made during an on-campus discussion group meeting. A would be agitator jumped on the moment with, "Yeah, right. The woman was talking to a snake. Like we can talk to snakes. This is just a myth that has been passed down through history. Gotta blame something, so why not a snake?"

> The discussion leader indulged the interruption and responded calmly with, "We can take that up as a full discussion topic at another time, but for now we can agree that the conflict between right and wrong began at some point and that God has always known about it. What is relevant for us today is that we know about it. And, not just know about it, but have a solution."

> The agitator accepted the statement and the discussion moved forward with how the Bible addressed situations and circumstances in today's world.

God created a perfect world and placed two perfect people in it. People, not robots. Adam and Eve had wills that responded to the influence of their intellect. Prior to an inappropriate response to their own intellectual capacity, there was no conflict in the world. Everything was in balance. I believe the created beings would have been able to communicate with one another. In that case it would not have been abnormal for Eve to talk with the other created beings, even a serpent. For the serpent to be overtaken by the spirit of Satan is totally abnormal. That Eve would succumb to a negative influence was known by God but not planned by God. Ol' what's his name developed and implemented the plan.

What Does That Make Him?

A liar, and the father of lies. All of the problems and negative situations affecting our lives today and throughout all history can be attributed to a lie and the furtherance of a massive untruth. The Apostle John recorded the words of Christ as He talked with the children of Abraham. He said, "You belong to your father, the Devil, and you want to carry out your father's desire. He was a murderer from the beginning, not holding to the truth, for there is no truth in him. When he lies, he speaks his native language, for he is a liar and the father of lies." [2] If the family of God could grab hold of this truth and spread it throughout the world, most of the problems we have today would become non-existent. We have the truth. We just need to share it.

What Did Adam And Eve Do?

Satan had a plan and knew what he was doing. He just needed to plant a seed of doubt into the mind of one of God's perfect people. His plan worked. He communicated with Eve and planted the seed. All he needed to do then was wait for it to grow. Scripture completes this story. "When the woman saw that the fruit of the tree was good for food and pleasing to the eye, and also desirable for gaining wisdom, she took some and ate it . . . ." [3] She gave in to the temptation. We can always ask why? Maybe it was pressure. Perhaps simple curiosity. Whatever the reason, she succumbed to a lie.

And Adam followed her in the act. ". . . She also gave some to her husband, who was with her, and he ate it." [3] Make sure you grasp this statement from the Word of God; Adam was "with" her.

There are those who say Adam was obeying God when he ate the forbidden fruit. Had not God told him to be fruitful and replenish the earth? They ask the question: How could Adam do this if he were not like Eve? This is a false teaching. They call it the commission of a lesser sin, in order to obey a greater commandment. The problem with any understanding like this is it only works if God is a liar. Who is the father of lies? Adam should have trusted God. Eve should have trusted Adam, and both of them should have said no. (If Adam was obeying God, why did God punish them with banishment?)

Then What Did They Do?

Look into a mirror. Search our own hearts. We are very much like Adam and Eve. We even look like them. And, since we come to where we are through them, we can pretty much share what went on in their life once they became self aware. They became ashamed and afraid. Not of their nakedness, but because of their nakedness. Before "the sin" they did not know about nakedness. "Then the eyes of both of them were opened, and they realized they were naked; so they sewed fig leaves together and made coverings for themselves."[4] They were somewhat resourceful.

They became pro-active about their situation, but they were still afraid. "Then the man and his wife heard the sound of the Lord God as He was walking in the garden in the cool of the day, and they hid from the Lord God among the trees of the garden."[5] The God of creation "walked in the garden" where Adam and Eve lived. We know from Scripture that no man has seen God in His true form. Scripture says that Jehovah "appeared" to Abram. In what form we do not know. (cf. Genesis 12:7; 17:1; 18:1, etc.) Evidence of His presence for sure, but not Him. Adam and Eve had the opportunity of actually hearing His sound as He walked in the midst of His creation, and they hid themselves.

Why?

Both Adam and Eve were afraid. When God called out to them, Adam answered, "I heard you in the garden, and I was afraid because I was naked; so I hid." [7] Neither of them could deal with their new condition. God called to them. Not because He didn't know where they were, or what they had done, but because He wanted them to know where "they" were. Something had happened with them and now their relationship with God had changed. They now were afraid of the very God who had created them.

Where Did That Leave Us?

God could have called for a "mulligan" or a "do over" and simply reset the universe. He chose to not do that. He was with the first man and woman on the earth and He knew going in what was ahead for them. So the teaching continued and the learning began.

God wanted to hear from Adam so He asked him what happened. Like most men today, Adam wanted to pass, or at least share the blame with someone else. According to Adam it was Eve's fault. When God asked Eve a similar question, her answer was predicable as well: The Devil made me do it.

Since we are all descendants of Adam and Eve, we are directly in line to receive whatever it is that God gave to them as a result of their inability to keep God's commandment. To Eve He said, ". . . I will greatly increase your pains in childbearing; with pain you will give birth to children. Your desire will be for your husband, and he will rule over you." [7] And to Adam He said, ". . . Because you listened to your wife and ate from the tree about which I commanded you, 'You must not eat of it,' cursed is the ground because of you; through painful toil you will eat of it all the days of your life.'" [8] Through

Adam and Eve we became part of the problem, and now share in the curse. God even cursed the serpent. The only remedy is God's way, and God's way is Jesus.

What Did God Do?

God is omniscient and knows what the outcome will be before commencement. He knew that in accordance with His will blood would be required to put things right. As He would in the future, God dealt with the problem personally. "The Lord God made garments of skin for Adam and his wife and clothed them. And the Lord God said, 'The man has now become like one of us, knowing good and evil. He must not be allowed to reach out his hand and take also from the tree of life and eat, and live forever.' So the Lord God banished him from the Garden of Eden to work the ground from which he had been taken." [9] You may want to mark this reference. It will come up again as we get into the work of sharing our faith and claiming Christ as Savior.

It isn't that God was so terribly mad and simply punished Adam and Eve, and us through them, He was more disappointed. The dispensation had changed and with it new rules. "After he drove the man out, he placed on the east side of the Garden of Eden cherubim and a flaming sword flashing back and forth to guard the way to the tree of life." [10] God saw to it that Adam and his descendents would have to look forward to find a way to enjoy an eternal relationship with Him. Denying them access to the tree of life left mankind with one option: God's way or no way.

Can We Identify With Adam And Eve?

Men and women of faith in today's world can identify with Adam and Eve. They were faced with a decision. They made it, albeit seriously wrong, and they had to live with it. God could look them in the eye and say with certainty that while He had not forgotten the incident, He could with equal certainty remember forgiving them. So, the natural question that comes from our looking back at the situation that so drastically impacted everyone, is: What would you have done in that situation? The answer is gender specific.

As a woman you must look at it from Eve's perspective. Eve saw that the fruit was good for food, and that it was pleasant to the eyes, and to be desired to make one wise. (cf. Genesis 3.6). Perhaps Eve thought the fruit to be endowed with all the gifts that life has to offer: It pleases the palate and satisfies hunger, it provides aesthetic pleasure, and it increases one's intellectual abilities. Eve may have envisioned the total range of the human experience, and, as Nehama Aschkenasy wrote in Eve's Journey, ". . . by eating the fruit she may have expressed a lust for life in all its manifestations. The act of violating God's command may have been the daring attempt of a curious person with an appetite for life to encompass the whole spectrum of life's possibilities." [a] In those exact circumstances, you might have responded differently. But, would you? Christ said, "Do not judge, or you too will be judged." [11]

As a man you must look at it from Adam's perspective. Adam was with Eve in the Garden of Eden. He knew well God's command to not partake of the forbidden fruit. God had created Adam and installed him as the leader of the first family on earth. Adam failed in this regard when he stood idly by and not only allowed Eve to be tempted by Satan, but allowed himself to be lead astray as well. In his book, Modern Manhood, Damon Cinaglia wrote, "Eve did not lead Adam into sin, rather he sinned on his own when he abdicated his position of headship over his wife" [b] So, under the same circumstance would you have acted differently? As a supposition, Adam did not want to live separated from Eve, but to be with her he had to go against God and he chose to do so.

Having made the analyses from both points of view, the follow-on question is: What should they have done? On this side of the event we might find ourselves a bit judgmental. After all, we have the benefit of 20-20 hindsight. But as believers and followers of Christ we can take an objective posture and present a solid response to the question. Adam and Eve, as well as ourselves if found in similar circumstances, should have: *Believed*—to demonstrate how we are to be saved; *Rebuked*—to demonstrate how we are to deal with Satan; *Trusted*—to demonstrate how we are to relate to God; *Accepted*—to demonstrate an appropriation of our faith; and *Acted*—to demonstrate that we are living for God. Ol' what's his name survived the Garden of Eden differently than Adam or Eve. He is alive and still out there lying to us and doing whatever he can to keep us from obeying God's modern day command to "go into all the world and make disciples."

Francis Schaeffer commented on the condition of Adam in <u>Basic Bible Studies</u>. "Adam was commanded to obey God and he sinned. (cf. Hebrews 2.3). We have all sinned. Therefore, we have earned spiritual, physical and eternal death. Now God in His love has given us another opportunity. This is not of works, but of grace, in which we partake if we accept His gift. If we accept Christ as our Savior and trust Him only for our salvation, if we believe on Him and accept His death for us, then we have eternal life. If we refuse God's gracious provision, we stay where we are, under the condemnation and judgment of God." [c]

What Are Some "Current-Day Lies" From Satan?

Whenever he can, and more particularly, whenever we allow him, Satan distorts the truth, defames our understanding of it, and just generally causes problems with our efforts to follow God's directions in witnessing. The Apostle John was on target when he quoted Christ saying, "he (Lucifer) is a liar and the father of lies." (cf. John 8.44). The following are a few of the current day lies Satan uses to confuse the effort:

- *You can't represent Jesus. You're not ready!*—Too many questions out there that you cannot answer. You will embarrass yourself and your church.
- *Surely you don't want to compromise Christ*—You give someone an incorrect answer and you could be responsible for them not becoming a believer and going to Hell.
- *Don't confront anyone, they might be offended*—You make someone uncomfortable by telling them they are lost, you could put yourself at risk and possibly make someone mad or upset, even an enemy.
- *You don't have to tell people about Jesus*—Jesus is God and He will save whomever He has chosen without your assistance. But, if someone comes to you, you might be able to encourage them in the Lord.
- *You will lose their friendship*—You've known Bill/Jill for years. He/she is a good person. If you push Jesus on him/her you could lose a longstanding friendship and hurt his/her feelings.
- *They will think you're a religious fanatic*—You know about those zealots who go into neighborhoods knocking on doors and passing out their literature. You don't want to get involved in anything like that.
- *You don't know enough Scripture*—You aren't up to snuff with your Bible memory work. You will fumble around trying

to repeat what you think is the correct verse and realize you have misquoted the passage.

- *It's not your place, someone else will do it*—Don't you remember the scripture verse where "some are called to be . . ." You weren't called. Someone else will go.
- *God can't use you as a witness*—Your life is too messed up. You've done too many bad things. People won't accept what you have to say because of what you have done.
- *They aren't going to accept Jesus anyway*—You know that God is not going to save everyone. Only those He has chosen will be saved. You can tell they won't accept Jesus.
- *Time just isn't right*—You will feel better about this later. When you've had more time to prepare. Right now just isn't right.
- *They will think you're strange*—People just don't talk about religion and stuff like that. You will be considered as some sort of odd-ball if you keep trying to talk about God stuff.
- *They may see your flaws*—You really aren't good enough to be a witness. You have no experience in sharing and besides, you really can't defend what you believe.

Any of these examples ring a bell? They, along with others, are out there all the time. We just have to continue believing the truth, work through them and get on with the task at hand: Telling others about the Lord and how they can have a personal relationship with Him. We must not allow Satan to have his way in our witness. The Apostle James wrote, "Resist the Devil, and he will flee from you." [12] One of the big things standing in our way is fear. Let's look at that.

God Didn't Give Us a Spirit of Fear

What is timidity (not shyness)? It is fear and disbelief. The Spirit of God will fill us with power, replace the fear and enable us to love and develop an attitude of self-discipline for our lives. The Apostle Paul in his second letter to Timothy wrote, "For God did not give us a spirit of timidity, but a spirit of power, of love and of self-discipline." [13]

The created cannot be greater than the Creator. Lucifer (aka Ol' what's his name) was created by God. Obviously the lesser. God's Word gives us authority over Satan's lies. Always remember: One with God is a majority. Paul asked the believers at Rome a specific question, "What, then, shall we say in response to this? If God is for us, who can be against us?" [14] God is the majority in and of Himself. We can be in the majority just by being with Him.

So, where does the strength come from? What can we do with it? Who says so? When questioned by the believers in Philippi, Paul said, "I can do everything through Him who gives me strength." [15]

We acknowledge Christ and God, through the Holy Spirit who lives in us and through that same Spirit we live in Him through Christ. We can rely on His love. In the first general epistle of the Apostle John, we can read, "If anyone acknowledges that Jesus is the Son of God, God lives in him and he in God. And so we know and rely on the love God has for us. God is love. Whoever lives in love lives in God, and God in him. In this way, love is made complete among us so that we will have confidence on the day of judgment, because in this world we are like Him. There is no fear in love. But perfect love drives out fear, because fear has to do with punishment. The one who fears is not made perfect in love." [16] The circuit is completed when we allow God's love to be lived through our lives. Because of this exchange, we can be confident of our destiny. We can love God, each other, and lost people, without fear. It's God's perfect love in action in this world.

The Psalmist David wrote, "The Lord is with me; I will not be afraid. What can man do to me?" [17] Sort of says it all. This fear thing is from Ol' what's his name. It is simply a message from Hell, trying to cut down the odds. Christ has won the battle. Satan is already defeated. There are still some skirmishes to keep the Saints busy until the Lord comes, but no man can keep us from doing what God has commanded His people to do: Go and share the "Good News."

I Didn't Witness When I Should Have, Now I . . .

"Ol' what's his name" will continue badgering us in any way we allow. It is just like him to take our less than stellar performance as witnesses for Christ and have us work through all types of negative thoughts. In that mind set we must deal with this open ended statement: I didn't witness when I should have, now I . . .

- **feel guilty, ashamed and defeated**—*God's Word says, "Do your best to present yourself to God as one approved, a workman who does not need to be ashamed and who correctly handles the word of truth."* [18]
- **won't receive my rewards in Heaven**—*God's Word says, ". . . because he is my disciple, I tell you the truth, he will certainly not lose his reward."* [19]
- **will suffer in my relationship with God**—*God's Word says, "For the Lord will not reject His people; He will never forsake His inheritance."* [20]
- **won't be able to share at all**—*God's Word says, ". . . do not throw away your confidence; it will be richly rewarded."* [21]
- **might as well forget about witnessing**—*God's Word says, "We are hard pressed on every side, but not crushed; perplexed, but not in despair."* [22]
- **just want to be left alone**—*God's Word says, "Never will I leave you. Never will I forsake you."* [23]
- **have to apologize to Jesus**—*God's Word says, "And we know that in all things God works for the good of those who love Him, who have been called according to His purpose."* [24]

Sharing God's truth is important work. Not witnessing when we feel urged to do so by the Holy Spirit should cause us some concern, but we have the unique position as believers of being able to pick ourselves up and get back at it. We must not allow Ol' what's his name any cause for applause. (This is one of the main reasons that we should not enter into a process of outreach or evangelism without a support group).

Claim the Victory and Press On

Being a witness is a post salvation experience. Satan did everything he could to keep you from accepting Christ, and now that you have, he will do whatever he can to mess with you and whatever you feel led to do in response to God's touch on your life. As a believer, you have the undisputed truth that Jesus has defeated Ol' what's his name. All you need to do is "claim the victory and press on." You start that process by telling the Devil to take a hike. There is no room for him in your life or in the life of anyone that God has brought to you for the Gospel message.

A significant and powerful method to use in dealing with the Devil is prayer. You should pray. Then pray some more. When you're done with that, pray some more. And, you should also pray with others. It's a reinforcing thing. You become stronger in your faith while you are encouraging another believer in theirs. Ol' what's his name is always blocked out when you are communicating with God. Our mediator is right there with God the Father representing us while we pray. Want to make the Devil mad? Then pray for his undoing. Pray for the ones to whom you are sharing the truth. Pray while you are going. Pray while you are there. And, pray while you are returning. Put a hedge of prayer around you and those for whom you are praying.

<u>Anecdote</u>: A young boy growing up in Texas remembers the times when a wonderful day of playing in a grassy field could turn into an extremely uncomfortable experience. Some of the fields, though inviting, were full of nettles, "stinging nettles." And to make it a bit more uncomfortable, some of the fields were bordered by pyracantha bushes. These large green bushes have twiny branches with lots of leaves and hundreds of long sharp thorns with a natural poison on their tips. Getting involved with either of these botanical variants can produce a painful memory. It can also paint a vivid picture of a prayer hedge. Give this a thought.

You have found a place where you can come and pray. It is quiet, somewhat remote, and around you God has grown this hedge of stinging nettles and pyracantha. You have come to pray and as you begin you become aware of something, or someone, trying to break through your prayer hedge. It's one of Ol' what's his name's demons and you have no time for this type of interruption. But wait a minute. Ol' what's his name's guy is on the outside of the hedge. To get to you he must come through the hedge of stinging nettles and pyracantha thorns. Not such a good thing for him. You can just continue with your prayers and trust that the hedge God has thrown up around you will provide all the protection you need.

While you pray, Lucifer's agent, in keeping with his persistent nature, continues to thrash his way into the hedge, attempting to reach your prayer center before you can complete your special time with the Lord. Just as your prayers are complete, the power of darkness pushes through the last part of the hedge. At that instant God lifts you up and the emissary of Satan is left alone inside the hedge. Now here's the good part.

Not only is "Ol' what's his name's" guy alone, he is "inside" the hedge. He could not penetrate the hedge while it protected you, but now he is inside and to get out he has to go back through the stinging nettles and pyracantha thorns, just to harass another believer. You would think "Ol' what's name" and his demons would learn that they cannot approach us when we are at prayer with our Savior and Lord.

Another part of the victory is sharing it with another believer. The contagious positive attitude of one believer to another is a wonderful experience. If you do not have a prayer partner, find one. Ask a brother/sister in the Lord to share the victory with you. It is even better if that person is also a friend. You know, someone you can count on. The Devil has an uncanny knack of attacking us at inconvenient times and a friend will not be easily dissuaded from coming to your side when the need arises. And if you team with a friend for witnessing, you have a natural check and balance when it comes to nurturing and helping new believers to grow in the Lord.

Accountability is also an important part of claiming the victory. The Apostle Paul was accountable to those who sent him. He also had accountability with those that went with him. In the Acts of the Apostles, Doctor Luke wrote ". . . they (Paul, Silas and Barnabas) gathered the church together and reported all that God had done through them and how He had opened the door of faith . . ."[25] When you are accountable to, or have another believer accountable to you, your witnessing efforts are more directed. With accountability you are able to more appropriately plan and then discuss the results of your actions. Accountability also gives you another level of protection from Ol' what's his name and makes it more difficult for him to have the opportunity of attacking you individually. If you do not have an accountability factor associated with your witnessing, you should seriously consider establishing a relationship with another believer that will provide this important element to your ministry.

With accountability comes a working understanding of your faith. You are saved. If that fact is a recent experience in your life, you are very close to what you felt at the moment you accepted Christ as your personal Lord and Savior. If that life changing experience occurred some time ago, you need to recapture the moment and become prepared to share the truth that lives within you. Being prepared to share involves knowing something about the faith that supports your testimony. You need to keep in mind what the Apostle Peter said in his first general epistle. "Always be prepared to give an answer to everyone who asks you to give the reason for the hope that you have." [26] A working understanding of your faith is part of the minimum requirements for sharing the "Good News."

One of the better ways to demonstrate the victory you have over the Devil and his influence on your life is to associate with and be seen in the company of brothers and sisters in Christ. People of faith should cultivate relationships with other people of faith. We are reinforced in our faith by walking the tough roads of life with others. When nonbelievers observe our fellowship they see Christ's love being shared. They may even become curious and ask us about our faith and what it is we have in common with these other people. In the process we are strengthened in our walk with the Lord and we can encourage one another in witnessing and sharing the truth as we live our lives in front of those who have yet to come to a realization that eternity is going to present an extremely lonely existence, without Christ.

And, when you are claiming the victory you should take it a day at a time. We all need to be out there, but we need to "grow" with God. It may be in "baby steps" at first, but we do not need to be running ahead of where we are. And, certainly not ahead of God. Patience is often an underused approach when getting involved with outreach. Excitement runs high and we want to "get out there" and be part of the doing. And we want to do it right now. The writer of Ecclesiastes put patience in perspective when he wrote, "The end of a matter is better than its beginning, and patience is better than pride." [27] If we take the time to grow into our position we will experience greater success as we press on with the work before us.

A fellow believer and I were involved in neighborhood evangelism. We used "water starts" from the local municipality to identify new residents in the vicinity of our church. With this information we could knock on the door and actually ask if a particular person was there. Our excitement peaked as we approached the front door of a particular residence. When the door opened we identified ourselves and inquired as to whether or not the particular individual was available. To our surprise, the door was flung open and we were asked to come in. We were not only "out there," we were *"in there."* Certainly an objective, but usually there is some exchange of information at the door. Not this time. We were inside the home with the residents with only a door knock and a "hi there!" What ensued is the rest of the story.

These folks were new to the city. They had no friends as yet. No church and no real interest in spiritual things. But, they were happy to see us. They wanted to know how we knew their name and why we had come to their home. We told them how we came by their name and that we were from a neighborhood church. We wanted to welcome them to the community and invite them to worship God with us at the church. They wanted to know about our church, so we told them. Then it was our turn to ask a few questions.

We presented the Gospel and asked each of them if there was any reason for them not to accept God at His word. No was their answer.

Each one responded yes to our question, did they wish to receive Christ into their lives then and there? We prayed with them and each one made a profession of faith. Ever heard of joy unspeakable? We were in a house full of it. We stayed with them for a while longer. We made arrangements for them to be with us in Church the next Sunday. We prayed with them again and then left the house.

Outside the house we claimed the victory. God had prepared the hearts and minds of those folks and we had just been used by God to deliver the message of truth to them. And, in God's perfect timing, and in His will, they were saved and became part of the forever family. We had grown up in our own faith. We had been faithful to God's call on our lives and He delivered on His promise. Now we had to help these folks grow in their own new found faith.

Where Does God Say "We" Save Anyone.

Many folks involved in outreach succumb to personality and technique clicks. After a few sashays around the block in this mode, we are susceptible to another trick of Ol' what's his name: Who did you save today? You would be wrong in whatever answer you give unless you acknowledge that you didn't save anyone. God does the saving. God simply says we are to witness. For sure, the telling is an important part of the process, but telling is all we can do. God draws unbelievers to Himself. As the Apostle John wrote when he recorded the words of Christ, ". . . no one can come to Me unless the Father has enabled him."[28] The Holy Spirit convicts them of their lost and sinful nature and the Lord Jesus Christ is their Savior.

Learning how to tell and being able to tell is our responsibility. God has arranged for believers to be the only conduit for a lost and dying world to hear the truth and see God's people in action getting the word out. Outreach is His business. We are simply privileged to be part of it. He is in charge of the "saving." We do the "telling."

Basically it comes down to following the directions. We are called by God. He has given us instructions and we have the responsibility of going about the work of reaching out to the lost in our neighborhoods, in our communities, in our country and around the world. We can attempt to do it on our own or submit to a process of growth and accountability. We will make mistakes, but we will learn and as we do the opportunities will increase. We need to keep our minds and hearts in tune with what God wants, and when all else fails, follow the directions.

"Ol' What's His Name" Will Do Anything.

If you have already experienced the excitement and reward associated with witnessing to those whom God has placed in your path, there is a good possibility you have experienced some interference from "Ol' what's his name" When you are in the process of stepping out in faith and become involved at some level in evangelism and outreach, you will be exposed to the emissaries of the Devil and they will do whatever they can to restrict your involvement.

The Devil and his crew will set you up with an arsenal of excuses. You can be planning an evangelism outing and myriad excuses may flood your mind. They will just come at you and when they get to working on you, it will be in an area of your walk with God where any excuse will do. You will still be sincere in your desire to witness, but the Devil works overtime when he sees a glimmer of hope that he can dissuade you from being involved.

Lucifer will even expose you to influenzas and common colds in an attempt to keep you from witnessing. All of the infections and diseases afflicting us today have developed as a result of man's separation from God through sin. "Ol' what's his name" was there then and he is here now. Just when you are on top of your game, you wake up with a fever on the very day you are scheduled to be part of a witnessing team going out from your church. God allows these trials, but the Devil orchestrates them. And, of course no one expects or wants you to go out when you are ill. Someone contracts your illness and look who gets the blame: God.

Oh, and of course there is always the situation that affects everyone: There just isn't enough time. You have your work and all that it involves. Then there is the special group function at the church. Your family is involved in so many extra-curricular activities. The special function you have been planning. Whatever it is, it is monopolizing your time and the one behind all this time consuming activity is none else than "Ol' what's his name." He doesn't have to worry about someone becoming involved in outreach if he can get that person inundated with time crunching activities.

Satan will also encourage you in your effort to cultivate an independent attitude. When you are independent, i.e., non-dependent, you are ripe for the destruction of your commitment to reach the lost among us. "Ol' what's his name" will applaud while you become more and more convinced that you have it all together and if someone will just ask, you are ready to impart your spiel about what it means to be saved. The Devil gets a good kick out of that. He doesn't want any believer to come together with other believers and find a way to bind him and keep him at bay while the work of witness is getting done.

There was a time, early in my Christian walk, when I thought I was God's gift to evangelism. I was definitely excited whenever I had a chance to share my faith with non-believers, but I was even more excited when I could share my outreach techniques and witnessing philosophies with other believers. Somehow I got confused about who I was opposed to whose I was. I had come to a self-proclaimed position of knowing just what to say in just about any witnessing situation. And, I enjoyed telling others where they could improve and where I thought they had gone off-track. Sometimes, perhaps most times, I did this without being asked. It wasn't that I didn't want others to be successful in their witnessing, I just wanted to be at the center of it. Especially in my group of enthusiastic evangelists at my church. Praise God He didn't allow this attitude to permeate me completely or to last for any significant length of time.

A Godly man at my church who was part of the outreach team had observed my aggressiveness in the work we were doing together. He was willing to let me learn rather than make me learn the hard way that God doesn't need any self-absorbed egomaniacal evangelistic zealot running anything. He kept an eye on me. He encouraged me to be more like Christ in my relationship with other believers. He also held me accountable and when I started making excuses about whatever or whoever it was that I thought was wrong, he focused on the Word of God to get my attention. "Humble pie is usually baked at home and better if eaten in private," is something he taught me. He also put me in touch with a special passage of Scripture. The Apostle Paul, in writing to the Romans had much to say about personal development. One thing he said was pointed out to me by my faithful brother in Christ, "For by the grace given me I say to every one of you: Do not think of yourself more highly than you ought, but rather think of yourself with sober judgment, in accordance with the measure of faith God has given you." [29]

Reviewing this Scripture, along with a multitude of correlating passages, provided the personal conviction necessary for me to abandon any course of action I was using, or the development of other less impressive attributes associated with self-laudatory acclamations. I surrendered all that I am or ever hope to be in this thing called life to Jesus Christ and have from that moment forward attempted to be transparent so that if applause is directed toward any of my involvement in outreach, witnessing and evangelism, it is for Him. And, with that statement I am even more committed to the principal that evangelism, in all its forms, is a "we" not an "I" endeavor.

Perhaps the most interruptive element in Satan's arsenal is his over-active involvement in our state of mind. He will do and use anything to mess with your head and cause you to be confused. Second guessing yourself is a common malady for any program or process which requires a personal commitment and follow-through. If even the slightest twinge of confusion is put into the mix, our effectiveness is affected. Paul was straight forward and to the point when he wrote in his first letter to the believers at Corinth, ". . . God is not a God of disorder but of peace." [30] Paul was talking about confusion and the fact that God doesn't cause it. Ol' what's his name invades our psyche and we come away with doubt and confusion.

We need to recognize and remember that the Devil will do anything to impede our progress as witnesses for the truth about what Jesus Christ has done for the entire creation of mankind. We must, as Paul put it in his letter to the Ephesians, "Put on the full armor of God so that you can take your stand against the Devil's schemes." [31] We know that ". . . in all things God works for the good of those who love Him, who have been called according to his purpose." [32] It's a *claim it* thing that all believers must do. The Devil can have access to us and our minds if we simply talk the talk but do not walk the walk. We can, and most assuredly should, rebuke the Devil in Jesus' name and Ol' what's his name will have no choice but to flee from us. God's word is specific in this. "Submit yourselves, then, to God. Resist the Devil, and he will flee from you." [33]

Questions

Trying to qualify or quantify the entity of Satan is not an enjoyable undertaking. Perhaps the following questions will stimulate your own search for the truth related to Ol' what's his name.

Who is "this Satan guy?"

Satan was once an angel. In fact, some theologians venture that he was the highest ranked angel of all the angels. His name was Lucifer. Lucifer means, "son of the morning star." He was highly favored by God. (d)

Lucifer was the Anointed Cherub. Anointed means to be set apart for God's divine purpose. It also means "bestowal of God's divine favor," and "appointment to a special place or function." God had given Satan a certain amount of power and authority. But he perverted that power. Lucifer wanted to exalt himself above God, . . . rather than "just" being the Angel of God. (e)

You know, Satan is really clever. He gets into the churches—in fact, he goes to church every Sunday and he majors in sowing discord. He may cause you to feel neglected and unappreciated. Oh, how subtle that is. And how satanic it is! That is the lie which began in heaven among the angels—(f)

Why did God create Satan?

God did not create the Devil. He created Lucifer, the star of the morning, a beautiful creature filled with wisdom . . . . But by his own volition, in his amazing beauty and wisdom, Lucifer said "I will . . ." five times. His desire was to rise up to be as the Most High.

What's more, he was able to convince one third of the angels to take his side against God. [g]

When did God create Satan?

Again, God did not create the Devil. The Cherub Angel who became Satan was created during God's program and process of creation. In Paul's letter to the believers at Colosse he wrote, "For by Him all things were created: things in heaven and on earth, visible and invisible, whether thrones or powers or rulers or authorities; all things were created by Him and for Him." [34]

Aren't Jesus and Lucifer brothers?

The Bible does not teach this, nor hint at it, nor even leave the door open for it to be a possibility. The Bible is very clear about who Jesus is. He is the one who created everything—including the angels. That includes Lucifer, who was an angel. (cf. Colossians 1.16). Jesus created everything, both in heaven and on earth, and that includes the angels. Lucifer was a cherub, which is a type of warrior angel. Ezekiel 28:13-19 describes Lucifer as being in the garden with God. Lucifer was a model of perfection. He was beautiful and "blameless in his ways"—meaning that he obeyed God perfectly. But then he was found to have wickedness in him, resulting from his vanity over his beauty, and God expelled him from the garden. Jesus is the creator. Lucifer is created. They cannot be brothers. [h]

What about those who claim to be atheists?

Claiming and being are two distinct positions. Rebellion is part of getting to a place where simply denying God becomes a way to eliminate any responsibility for having rejected the truth and taking the extremely weak point of view that there is no God. Ray Comfort, in his book <u>God Does Not Believe in Atheists</u>, made a strong statement concerning this issue.

"To say categorically, 'There is no God,' is to make an absolute statement. For the statement to be true, I must know for certain that there is no God in the entire universe. No human being has all knowledge; therefore none of us is able to truthfully make the assertion.

If you insist upon disbelief in God, what you must say is 'Having the limited knowledge I have at present, I believe that there is no God.' Owing to a lack of knowledge on your part, you don't know if God exists; so in the strict sense of the word, you cannot be an atheist. The only true qualifier for the title is the One who has absolute knowledge . . . and why on earth would God want to deny His own existence?" [i]

CHAPTER FIVE

SHOW YOURSELF APPROVED

You Are Christ's Representative

Know What God Says About:

Study—Pray—Study—Pray. You should:

Be Ready

Share the Experience

Declare and Demonstrate the Fruit of the Spirit

Put It in Your Heart Where Your Mind Can Find It

Know Where You Are

Know When to Quit

Sample Questions—Not Stock Spiel

Questions

B ecoming a born again Christian is the most important step anyone can take during a person's natural life on earth. Dwell on that statement for a moment. There are multiple wonderful and memorable moments in everyone's life. Even so, there is a "once-in-a-lifetime" moment that cannot be participated in with another person: Salvation. It is innately personal, and, as great as some of our moments are, they pale when compared to that moment when you took God at His word and traded all that you were for all that Christ is and has done for you, and accepted Him as your personal Lord and Savior. You can tell others about it but you cannot experience it for another person. With that decision made, we are to follow God's directives while we maintain our physical position in God's forever family. As witnesses for Christ we should do the work and show ourselves approved.

You Are Christ's Representative

As ambassadors for Christ, we know it is our responsibility to share the truth and spread the Gospel. Being prepared to step forward in faith is part of that responsibility. This concept was important enough for the Apostle Paul to have mentioned it to the Believers at Corinth. In his second letter to them he wrote, "We are therefore Christ's ambassadors, as though God were making his appeal through us. We implore you on Christ's behalf: Be reconciled to God." [1] We are all "works in progress" and like any station in life, you get from something in direct proportion to the effort contributed.

As Christ's representatives we should have our act together, so to speak, and know what has happened in our own life so that when an opportunity is presented we will be in a good position to share the truth that lives within us. Getting our thoughts organized around our own salvation experience is a good way to become comfortable with who we are in Christ. You can structure your thoughts in any manner that works for you. The following "step-plan" may help to get the juices flowing:

Step 1—**Believe**. This is how you were saved. God's Word says, ". . . if you confess with your mouth, 'Jesus is Lord,' and believe in your heart that God raised him from the dead, you will be saved."[2] Having done this you are set for the next step.

Step 2—**Rebuke**. This is how you deal with Satan. God's Word says, "Submit yourselves, then, to God. Resist the Devil, and he will flee from you."[3] Ol' what's his name will come at you from any direction. Claim the promise of God's Word and press on.

Step 3—**Trust**. This is how you relate to God. God's Word says, "Trust in the Lord with all your heart and lean not on your own understanding,"[4] Our walk with God is a "faith walk." Trusting God to do what He has said He will do is a very large part of a relationship with Him.

Step 4—**Accept**. This is how you appropriate your position in Christ. God's Word says, "And we also thank God continually because, when you received the Word of God, . . . you accepted it not as the word of men, but as it actually is, the Word of God, which is at work in you who believe."[5] As believers, we take in the truth and make it part of ourselves. God's truth lives in and flows out through us.

Step 5—**Act**. This is how you live for Christ. God's Word says, ". . . someone will say, 'You have faith; I have deeds.' Show me your faith without deeds, and I will show you my faith by what I do."[6] We are doing what God has directed because of our faith, not to obtain our faith.

Mark McCloskey, in his book Tell It Often Tell It Well, suggesting that we make the most of witness opportunities wrote, "New

Testament evangelism was accomplished by men and women who were[are] spiritually in tune with their Lord and, therefore, ready at any moment to be used by God in the work of being witnesses to the gospel. We may not all be used in the radical way that [the Disciple] Stephen was but witnessing opportunities are there [here] for the one who is spiritually prepared to make the most of them (cf. Colossians 4.5-6). Ephesians 5.18 commands us to be 'filled with the Spirit.' We are to walk in the light as He is in the light (cf.1 John 1.7). Our attitude of availability needs to be in the context of our being filled with the Spirit, for we must be equipped with God' power through the Holy Spirit inn order to engage in spiritual battle. [a]

Know What God Says About:

If you can count to one, (raise your index finger), you can identify the way of salvation: **Jesus**. If you can count to five, (the number of fingers on your hand), you can make a fist. And, like a bundle of twigs being more difficult to break when they are tied together than when they are a single "stand alone" twig, you have five main points you can make in presenting the truth, or defending your faith. You can fold almost any presentation of the Gospel around these points. You should take the time to know what God says about:

1. **Man's Position**—Everyone you know, or meet, is either born again or not. Through the failure of Adam and Eve all mankind has inherited the position of needing to accept God on His terms rather than on some set of self-contrived rules, edicts, mantra, or other "man sponsored" program of religiosity. The Holy Spirit directed the prophet Isaiah to write, "We all, like sheep, have gone astray, each of us has turned to his own way . . ." [7] As true today as at the time of the writing.

From the earliest time in man's existence, we have been involved with our sin nature. The Apostle Paul wrote to the Romans about this very thing. "As it is written: 'There is no one righteous, not even one; there is no one who understands, no one who seeks God. All have turned away, they have together become worthless; there is no one who does good, not even one.'" [8] All mankind is in this condition today. We are by our very nature, sinners.

Mankind, without a personal relationship with God is condemned to an earthly and eternal existence separated from God. Moses' account of our history makes this perfectly clear. In his Book of the Beginnings, he wrote, "The Lord God took the man and put him in the Garden of Eden to work it and take care of it. And the Lord God commanded the man, 'You are free to eat from any tree in the garden; but you must not eat from the tree of the knowledge of good and evil, for when you eat of it you will surely die.'" [9] In this example, die means to be separated from God. Adam ate the forbidden fruit and suffered for it. Ultimately he did die a physical death, but for his "sin" he had to endure being separated from God. Adam set the bar for all of us. And, he set it so high no one but God could get over it.

God took control of the situation that had developed with His creation. He was absolutely specific when it came to the penalty for disobeying His Commandment. The Apostle Paul, in his letter to the Romans, made it very clear as to the consequences associated with mankind's natural inclination toward sin. "For the wages of sin is death . . ." [10] Even with the assurance of Paul's closing statement, ". . . but the gift of God is eternal life in Christ Jesus our Lord," [10] mankind is still under the penalty of death for having not trusted God, and disobeying His commandment.

Mankind, attempting to set aside the penalty prescribed by God, has spent a large amount of the ensuing time since Adam committed the original sin, trying to dispel the truth and discredit the idea of God being the Supreme Being. Mankind has been working hard in the laboratory and finding ways to prove beyond any shadow of doubt that, "Although they claimed to be wise, they became fools." [11] This is called intellectual suicide and is practiced by all those who have followed Adam by inheriting his sin and refusing to accept Christ as their Savior.

2. *God's Position*—The Prophet Jeremiah left his mark in Scripture and following the inspiration of the Holy Spirit wrote, "This is what the Lord says: 'If those who do not deserve to drink the cup must drink it, why should you go unpunished? You will not go unpunished, but must drink it.'" [12] Pretty much puts a lid on it that only God can remove. He will not allow anyone to escape the penalty of physical death.

Mankind must accept and understand that the created are not and can never be as great as the Creator. This should be an intuitive understanding, but somehow who God is gets confused in the minds of those who are looking for a created being to fill in all the blanks. John, a man who walked with Christ, knew the importance of knowing who God is. In his gospel he wrote, "God is Spirit, and His worshipers must worship in spirit and in truth." [13] All who would come to GOD need to understand first that the things of God are spiritually discerned before they can be personally applied.

God is just and Holy. In his time, the prophet Isaiah wrote about the deliverance and restoration of Israel. He quoted God when he penned, ". . . there is no God apart from me, a righteous God and a Savior; there is none but Me." [14] God does not share his position. He shares His truth. Being just, He established the standard for righteousness. And, being Holy, He provided Himself as Savior to any of His creation who would accept Him.

God is Sovereign. Instructed by God, Isaiah also wrote, "This is what the Lord says—Israel's King and Redeemer, the Lord Almighty: 'I am the first and I am the last; apart from Me there is no God.'" [15] One God and one way to access Him: Jesus, the first and the last (cf. Revelation 22.13). Today, just as it was in the eighth century B.C., God provides the way for His own to know Him and to be part of His forever family.

The Apostle Peter expressed God's desire for His entire creation. In his second general epistle, he wrote, "The Lord is not slow in keeping His promise, as some understand slowness. He is patient . . . , not wanting anyone to perish, but everyone to come to repentance." [16] When God says "everyone" He means everyone. And, everyone means "everyone who will" accept the truth and come to God in faith, believing.

3. *The Word*—The Apostle Paul wrote about the Word of God in his letter to the believers in Rome. They, not unlike believers today, had questions and Paul wrote, "For everything that was written in the past was written to teach us, so that through endurance and the encouragement of the Scriptures we might have hope." [17] Writing down an important concept is more secure than surrendering it to a spoken comment that may become confused as it is passed along to others. God used the "pen" in the hands of His chosen emissaries to reduce a few of His pertinent thoughts to writing. The written word can be reviewed and examined. If you want it to last, write it down. God wrote His Word down and He doesn't need to write it again. We just need to read and apply it to our lives today.

God's Word is Scripture. And, as Paul wrote in his second letter to Timothy, "All Scripture is God-breathed and is useful for teaching, rebuking, correcting and training in righteousness, so that the man of God may be thoroughly equipped for every good work." [18] The Word is communication of God's truth for us, direct from the Source.

God's Word is powerful. The Apostle John recorded the words of Jesus as He told those who believed in Him about the Word. Jesus said, ". . . If you hold to My teaching, you are really My disciples. Then you will know the truth, and the truth will set you free." [19] God's Word is most certainly truth and we have, on the authority of Christ Himself, the ability to absorb it and use its power in our lives today.

God's Word has eternal worth. When you think about the Word of God having been available for centuries, it won't be very difficult to consider it will continue being available for any centuries that may come. The prophet Isaiah presented God's thought about this concept when he wrote, "The grass withers and the flowers fall, but the Word of our God stands forever." [20] This gives us the comfort of knowing we will always have God's written word, today and throughout eternity.

God's Word has a purpose. You wouldn't write a personal message to someone you love, without a purpose. And, God certainly didn't write His message for those He loves without reason or a purpose. He confirmed this through His Apostle John, who wrote in his first general epistle, "I write these things to you who believe in the name of the Son of God so that you may know that you have eternal life." [21] You might want to memorize or mark this verse for a quick reference, especially when you want to share this fact with someone.

4. *Who is Jesus?*—The Apostle John began his writing with, "In the beginning was the Word, and the Word was with God, and the Word was God. He was with God in the beginning." [22] This is the same beginning as written in Genesis, "In the beginning God created the heaven and the earth." [23] The Prophet Samuel wrote about a prayer of Hannah, who prayed, ". . . those who oppose the Lord will be shattered. He will thunder against them from heaven; the Lord will judge the ends of the earth. He will give strength to his King and exalt the horn of

his Anointed." [24] Anointed in this verse is translated "Christ" and is the first mentioning of the Messiah in Scripture. Any serious examination of God's Word affirms that Jesus is God.

I encounter the question as to who Jesus is on a regular basis. Non-believers, as well as those who have bought in to false teaching and poor eschatology, have difficulty accepting Him as God. Part of sharing the truth of Christ is sharing His role in the Godhead. I stay with the Word of God and never argue the point. If the person to whom a witness is given accepts Christ, He will take control of the situation through the power of the Holy Spirit and that person will come to know the full truth as to who Jesus is.

God leaves no doubt as to who Jesus is. His Word, through the Prophet Isaiah, credits God as the One who named and identified Jesus before His earthly existence. "For to us a child is born, to us a Son is given, and the government will be on His shoulders. And He will be called Wonderful Counselor, Mighty God, Everlasting Father, Prince of Peace." [25] God knew the plan of salvation before Adam fell from grace. From the beginning, God was not asking mankind to do something He had not done or would not do Himself. Before Jesus was born as a babe, Adam and all who followed him, could look forward to what would be done. All who have come into existence since Christ's birth, death and resurrection, can look at the actual fact of God's truth and promise.

From the beginning, God knew there would be confusion and misunderstandings about His plan. He told of, and then true to His Word, He provided a way for all to know the plan and how to be part of it. In his gospel, the Apostle John recorded a conversation between Thomas, a disciple and the Lord Jesus Christ. Thomas had specifically asked Jesus how they could know the way and Jesus answered, ". . . I am the way and the truth and the life. No one comes to the Father except through Me." [26]

Anecdote: Consider someone who is physically lost. Perhaps on a long walk in the woods and they find themselves disoriented and darkness is about to come on them. Another person walks into the area and through an exchange of greetings understands the other person is lost. "Well then, it's a good thing I came along. Walk with me. I know the way to where you want to go." The lost person has a decision to make: Reject the offer and stay lost. Or, accept the offer and get home safely. Either way, there is some walking to do. One way is safe. The other is sorrow.

I remember being lost. I remember what it was like. How I felt and how desperate I was to find my way. I had been raised by good parents and had the example of a Godly mother. I had been in church and heard the Word of God preached by pastors and teachers, from my youth into adulthood, but I was lost. It wasn't until I was in a place that focused my attention on something other than myself that I was given the incentive to ask Christ to identify Himself and lead me home. He came alongside of me and walked me to the safety of eternal fellowship with Him.

As further evidence, Jesus Himself told the Jews in Jerusalem, "I and the Father are One." [27] The Jews didn't like that idea very much and, like many in the world today, vehemently rejected Him. The writer of Hebrews gives additional insight as to who Jesus is when he credits God, in referring to His Son as saying, ". . . Your throne, O God, will last for ever and ever, and righteousness will be the scepter of Your kingdom." [28]

The Prophet Isaiah, in writing about the deliverance and restoration of Israel, quoting God, as directed by the Holy Spirit, wrote, "You are My witnesses, . . . and My servant whom I have chosen, so that you may know and believe Me and understand that I am He. Before

Me no God was formed, nor will there be one after Me. I, even I, am the Lord, and apart from Me there is no Savior." [29] This is a reference to salvation and that there is no other God that will be our Savior. The Apostle John in his first general epistle to believers wrote, "My dear children, I write this to you so that you will not sin. But if anybody does sin, we have one who speaks to the Father in our defense—Jesus Christ, the Righteous One. He is the atoning sacrifice for our sins, and not only for ours but also for the sins of the whole world." [30] No one exposed to the truth can, in honest sincerity, deny that Jesus is our Savior; the One and only Savior for all times.

5. *Faith*—Like nothing else in the process of being saved, faith is the first step. Without faith you cannot believe, and without believing you cannot be saved. The writer of Hebrews gave us the definition of faith when he wrote, ". . . faith is being sure of what we hope for and certain of what we do not see." [31] Faith is the beginning of our life experience with Christ. It starts the process.

Once we come to Christ by faith, the next step in the process of salvation is accepting the fact that God, through His grace did the saving. The Apostle Paul made this fact perfectly clear for us and to the believers at Ephesus when he wrote, "For it is by grace you have been saved, through faith—and this not from yourselves, it is the gift of God—not by works, so that no one can boast." [32]

If someone should claim any responsibility other than the sharing of God's truth in someone's salvation experience, they would be grossly overstating their position. Paul also wrote to the believers in Corinth about living by faith. In his second letter to them he wrote, "We live by faith, not by sight." [33] Faith is a large part of the process of life.

And faith is our justification before the Lord. Paul wrote in his letter to the Romans, "For we maintain that a man is justified by faith apart from observing the law." [34] No one can keep the law. If we could, we could save ourselves. There would be no need for Christ to have died in our place. God could just sit back and encourage us to work out our own salvation. If we fall short, He could just banish us to the Lake of Fire.

Ray Comfort provided a succinct statement about Hell with his reference to the Law and its purpose in his book Hell's Best Kept Secret. He wrote, "The purpose of the Law is fourfold:

1. To show the world its *guilt* before God.
2. To give us the *knowledge* of sin.
3. To show us the *depth* of our sin.
4. To be a *schoolmaster* to lead us to Christ

We have seen that ignorance of the Law leaves the sinner careless about his soul. The good news of Calvary is foolishness to him. The only way to awaken him is to show him the divine Law and all its consequences for the guilty soul. Then and only then will he be brought to a place of despair and cry out for salvation. No wonder the preaching of the Law is Hell's best kept secret." [b]

None-the-less, we should be honoring our faith by doing the work God has called us to do. We should be demonstrative in our faith. We cannot work "for" our salvation but we most certainly can work "out of" our salvation. James, the brother of Christ, wrote, "What good is it, . . . if a man claims to have faith but has no deeds? Can such faith save him? Suppose a brother or sister is without clothes and daily food. If one of you says to him, 'Go, I wish you well; keep warm and well fed,' but does nothing about his physical needs, what good is it? In the same way, faith by itself, if it is not accompanied by action, is dead." [35] If we are not supposed to do anything with our faith, God would simply take us off the earth at the moment we came to Him in faith, accepted Christ as our savior and believed. We, like the New Testament era believers, need to be involved in God's work. Our faith should be active, not passive.

We have the assurance from Jesus Christ that we are joined to Him through the Holy Spirit. And, we also understand that with this indwelling power, we are still confronted with our natural inclinations. Even so, we are to surrender our will into God's hand. When we operate independent of the Holy Spirit's leading, we find ourselves in conflict with the best of what God wants for our lives.

In her book <u>The Person and Work of the Holy Spirit</u>, René Pache wrote the following about *Sanctification Through the Spirit*. "God can free me from sin and it is to this end that He places His Spirit in me. As soon as I no longer resist Him and surrender my own will, the Spirit fills and sanctifies me ever increasingly (cf. Romans 6.13). Nevertheless I remain free, but if my will ceases to be in submission then, immediately, the Spirit ceases His work. *(Still inborn and available, implied).* It must be further pointed out that such a halt in the Spirit's working is not brought about solely by an open act of rebellion of the will. It can be equally caused by that desire, that is so frequent, to fight with one's own power, seeking to manage one's own affairs without help, which is the characteristic mark of the carnal Christian. God intervenes to pardon, regenerate, and sanctify us only when we place ourselves in His hands that He alone might command, for He knows that no man will ever attain salvation and sanctification through his own endeavors." [c]

Study—Pray—Study—Pray. You should:

Showing yourself approved involves some work on your part. When you know that you know that you know, it's a normal step to position yourself as a witness. An important part of the process now is to balance your activity around time set aside for study and time set aside for prayer. It is sort of a by-the-numbers process:

1. **Study**—Study's primary objective is to look to the Word of God for inspiration and confirmation. In Paul's second letter to Timothy he encouraged Timothy to, "Do your best to present yourself to God as one approved, a workman who does not need to be ashamed and who correctly handles the word of truth." [36] This implies study. Get into the Word of God and make it part of your life.

Train Yourself to be Godly is an area of concern in Jerry Bridges book, The Practice of Godliness. He wrote, "Every Christian should be a student of the Bible. The [early] Hebrew Christians were rebuked, because although they should have been able to teach others they still needed to be taught the elementary truths of God's Word. They needed milk, not solid food! Unfortunately, many of us are like those Christians." [d]

2. **Pray**—Study comes with prayer. Paul communicated with the Philippians and in his writing to them he said, ". . . in everything, by prayer and petition, with thanksgiving, present your requests to God." [37] We should do no less when it comes to witnessing.

3. **Continue your study**—Even a casual reading of the Word of God exposes you to truth and wisdom that emanates from no other source. The writer of the Book of Ecclesiastes captured this sense of life when he wrote, "So I turned my mind to understand, to investigate and to search out wisdom and the scheme of things and to understand the stupidity of wickedness and the madness of folly." [38] We are in this thing called life with someone who is more than capable of directing us toward the truth and the ability to represent Him to the world around us.

4. **Never stop praying**—We are instructed to pray without ceasing. Paul wrote to the believers at Thessalonica and encouraged them to

"Pray continually." [39] As we prepare to witness, prayer is vital to our process of preparation.

Be Ready

If you are not "ready" to respond to an inquiry about your faith, it will be a disappointing experience. You will have missed an opportunity to share and the one who is asking will not hear the truth or receive an answer. The Apostle Peter addressed this in his first general epistle. He wrote, ". . . in your hearts set apart Christ as Lord. Always be prepared to give an answer to everyone who asks you to give the reason for the hope that you have. But do this with gentleness and respect, . . ." [40] To the point: Be ready. An uncomplicated system of thought could be developed around the following:

1. *Know what you know and say so*—You are where you are, and you are who you are. Get comfortable with yourself. You have the knowledge of your life through today. You are not witnessing to others on a whim. Those who ask are not requesting a sermon. They are simply curious. Maybe even seriously interested in what you have to say about your own spiritual development. You know what you know first hand. You won't be talking abstractly about your faith.

2. *Refresh your mind daily*—A few folks in this world awake every day renewed and refreshed, excited about the new day and are eager to get going immediately. The rest of us are more normal. We thank God for the new day, just like the effervescent few, but we need a few moments to compose ourselves and organize our thoughts around the purpose we will serve this day. We need to refresh our minds and spirits about the truth that resides within. With that done, we can get into whatever it is God has for us, knowing that we are ready.

3. *Practice—practice—practice*—Osmosis is not a method most of us use to become effectual at anything. Knowledge is only part of the process. It has to be applied, and the more we apply it, the more accomplished we become. Our "faith walk" becomes easier and more effective when we have done it before. And, the more often we become involved in sharing the better we get at doing it. Pick a friend to work with you. Practice your own personal method of sharing with each other. Group sessions are excellent opportunities to "hone" your skills in sharing Christ with others.

4. *Build your confidence*—Confidence is developed. You won't get it without some effort on your part. Witnessing once is a good thing. Witnessing twice is a better thing. And, it just keeps getting better as you go forward in witnessing. Think about it this way: The second try is the first step. It begins the process of building your confidence in preparation for multiple opportunities to share your faith. Each time you witness builds confidence for the next time God places you in a position to share your faith.

Share the Experience

Scripture shares many exciting and traumatic experiences with us. Moses could hold out his hand and part the *Red Sea*. (cf. Exodus 14.21). Elijah was taken up in a chariot of fire. (cf. 2 Kings 2.11). Enoch walked with God and was not. (cf. Genesis 5.23). Paul was struck blind by the power of the Holy Spirit. (cf. Acts 9.8). Peter stepped out of a boat and walked on water. (cf. Matthew 15.29). These and many other experiences are shared with us through Scripture. Even so, the one that is most important is experiencing salvation. The Apostle Paul shared his salvation experience with the believers at Corinth. In his first letter to them, he wrote, ". . . I want to remind you of the Gospel I preached to you, which you received and on which you have taken your stand. By this Gospel you are saved, if you hold firmly to the word I preached to you. Otherwise, you have believed in vain. For what I received I passed on to you as of first importance: that Christ died for our sins according to the Scriptures, that He was buried, that He was raised on the third day according to the Scriptures," [41] Paul declared salvation to be of "first importance."

If you have experienced the explicit blessing of having your name written in the Lamb's Book of Life, you most certainly would agree with Paul. And, when you ponder the effect, you might want to give some thought as to how you could share your experience with others. The following "three-point" process could be of assistance.

When you take a look at your own experience you should take some time and investigate your position with the following:

1. *What do you "really" feel about salvation?*—Use your own words. Don't rely on what you have heard someone else say, or what you have read that someone else has written. Listening and reading can easily be part of your research, but the answer to the question must come from you. Your words make it personal.

A believer has a personal position in their relationship with Christ. Take some time to think about yours. Jesus is very personal to you, and you are very personal to Him. When your thoughts are clear, write them down. Review them. Refine them. Make your thoughts about your own salvation experience part of you.

When you are talking with someone about your faith in Christ, or attempting to share what happened in your life when you were saved, you should:

2. *Relate your experience to whomever*—Be careful to not fabricate or embellish the circumstances associated with your salvation experience.

Your experience is uniquely yours. You do not need to stylize it or make any "out-of-sync" comments. God met you right where you were and when you accepted Christ, the deal was sealed.

Simply suggest an understanding of the circumstances as they existed at the specific time. Be specific and include any pertinent details. But remember, too many details and you will get lost in the presentation. If you are asked for the time you wouldn't tell the one asking how to build a watch. You were asked because you displayed the ability to provide an answer: You were wearing a watch.

3. *Earn the privilege of sharing your faith*—Set the tone of your position by presenting yourself in a non-threatening way. Ask questions in a gentle but sincere manner. It is similar to priming a water pump: Before you can get the pump to actually pump water, you need to give it some water. That action lubricates the glands in the pump and enables it to begin pumping out some new water. If you ask gentle questions that do not set-off the anti-God alarm, you may be given the opportunity of taking the conversation to a level where you can introduce the Gospel.

Don't get preachy either. You have a message they need to hear, but you won't get the chance to deliver it if you come at them with a preaching attitude. Preachers often times have a way of demonstrating a "holier than thou" attitude toward those who have yet to accept Christ. You can take them to a preacher in the event they want to go, but getting into a preaching mode could result in being ignored, or even ridiculed.

By asking appropriate or non-threatening questions and avoiding the temptation to pulpiteer, you will earn the privilege to share your salvation experience.

Declare and Demonstrate the Fruit of the Spirit

Any believer, new or seasoned, has, with some degree of certainty, been exposed to folks who claim a personal relationship with our Lord and Savior, when in reality, it is more "show" and less "go." God has plenty to say about being more than a non-bearing fruit tree. A good example of His position is expressed by Jesus Himself. The Apostle Matthew recorded the Savior telling the Pharisees, "Make a tree good and its fruit will be good, or make a tree bad and its fruit will be bad, for a tree is recognized by its fruit . . . . The good man brings good things out of the good stored up in him, and the evil man brings evil things out of the evil stored up in him." [42]

In teaching His disciples, Jesus also said, "By their fruit you will recognize them. Do people pick grapes from thorn bushes, or figs from thistles? Likewise every good tree bears good fruit, but a bad tree bears bad fruit. A good tree cannot bear bad fruit, and a bad tree cannot bear good fruit. Every tree that does not bear good fruit is cut down and thrown into the fire. Thus, by their fruit you will recognize them." [43]

In correlation, a pear tree cannot truly be a pear tree until it bears fruit and a person identifying him/herself as a Christian, cannot/ is not truly a Christian without producing evidence of that fact in their life.

Without debate, we are saved by the grace of God through faith. Christ alone is the husbandman that did all that was necessary for any believer to become part of God's forever family. And, like the pear tree, with the help of the husbandman, we are to grow and produce fruit. The Holy Spirit is the vine dresser and as believers we are to be filled with the Holy Spirit. The Apostle Paul, in his letter to the believers at Ephesus, along with encouraging them to adopt moderation regarding their drinking of wine, told them, ". . . to be filled with the Spirit." [44] Filled in this instance means to keep on being filled. Just as water is the life blood of a pear tree, so is the Holy Spirit a believer's living water that enables the development of fruit.

There is an unfounded school of thought prevalent in Christendom these days. This wayward thought suggests that accepting the position of "once saved always saved" allows a fruitless existence in a believer's life. It further suggests since eternal security is no longer a concern, that by simply saying the words "Jesus is Lord" (cf. Romans 10.9), one is saved and can live their life at any level and still gain Heaven at the end. "Whoa-up there pardoner," is what one of my dear friends and a fellow believer in Texas would say to that comment. That same referenced passage in God's Word also says, "and believe in your heart . . ." which introduces a more complete understanding of the responsibility on the part of a believer. When you hold something near enough that it becomes part of you, you pay attention to the nurturing and caretaking requirements associated with whatever you are holding. Salvation is without question very near and dear to anyone professing faith in the Lord Jesus Christ as their God breathed guarantee of eternal life.

There is a modern day heresy that has the audacity to suggest that Christians are above the law. Not just man's law, but God's law as well. R. C. Sproul, Sr. wrote about this condition in his book, Essentials of the Christian Faith. "There is an old rhyme that serves as something of an antinomian theme song. It says, 'Freed from the law, O blessed condition; I can sin all I want and still have remission.' [Cute little ditty, but most assuredly not correct] Antinomianism[*] literally means anti-lawism. It denies or downplays the significance

---

[*] Theologically, Antinomianism is the doctrine that by faith and God's grace, a Christian is freed from all laws, including the moral standards of the culture.

of God's law in the life of the believer. It is the opposite of its twin heresy, legalism.

Antinomians acquire their distaste for the law in a number of ways. Some believe that they no longer are obligated to keep the moral law of God because Jesus has freed them from it. They insist that grace not only frees us from the curse of God's law but delivers us from any obligation to obey God's law. Grace then becomes a license for disobedience.

Antinomianism's primary error is confusing justification with sanctification. We are justified by faith alone, apart from works. However, all believers grow in faith by keeping God's holy commands—not to gain God's favor, but out of loving gratitude for the grace already bestowed on them through the work of Christ." [e]

There are many folks in and of the world today who, having been exposed to the truth of Christ, made what all true believers consider to be the right or correct choice: Accept Christ and be saved. Then, for whatever reason, most probably because no one came alongside them to encourage and nurture their new position, they reverted to their pre-Christian lifestyle. Some may have made token efforts to be absorbed into the family of God, but, again, as circumstance may have dictated, they have not put a foot in the path, so to speak, toward producing any real fruit.

The Apostle Paul wrote to the Galatians about living life by the Spirit. He wrote, ". . . I say, live by the Spirit, and you will not gratify the desires of the sinful nature. For the sinful nature desires what is contrary to the Spirit, and the Spirit what is contrary to the sinful nature. They are in conflict with each other, so that you do not do what you want. But if you are led by the Spirit, you are not under law." [45]

There are also many folks today who have not developed any relationship with Christ beyond counting on a decision which has not matured with the production of any fruit in or from their life. Some are actually quite busy with activities they hope are good enough to convince Christ to welcome them with open arms into the Heavenly Kingdom when Day is done. Jesus has a direct and specific word for these folks. As recorded by Matthew, Christ said, "Not everyone who says to me, 'Lord, Lord,' will enter the kingdom of heaven, but only he who does the will of my Father who is in Heaven. Many will say to me on that day, 'Lord, Lord, did we not prophesy in your name, and in your name drive out demons and perform many miracles?' Then I will tell them plainly, 'I never knew you. Away from me, you evil doers!'" [46]

So, the question must be presented: If Jesus has lost none of those who the Father has given Him, (cf. John 17.24), how can one who has expressed belief and claimed salvation through the blood of Jesus be set aside on judgment day?[*] The Apostle Paul dealt with this question in his letter to the believers at Galatia, when he wrote, "The acts of the sinful nature are obvious: sexual immorality, impurity and debauchery; idolatry and witchcraft; hatred, discord, jealousy, fits of rage, selfish ambition, dissensions, factions and envy; drunkenness, orgies, and the like. I warn you, as I did before, that those who live like this will not inherit the kingdom of God." [47] Paul did not restrict these comments to just the non-believers of his day. He was aware then as we are today, there are those who profess to believe in Jesus Christ, and with their mouth confess that He is Lord, and yet they still live unrepentant lives in disregard of the truth they attempt to profess. We all know some of those non-spiritual, fruitless folks, even

---

[*] An essential element of faith is understanding that God knows His own and has pre-selected everyone that will be saved and gives custody of them to Jesus. The Apostle John recorded this truth so that God's Word would be available to address this question.

if that fact is quietly held in our thoughts fruitless folks, even if that fact is quietly held in our thoughts.

Anecdote: Tim (not his actual name) has been a self-professed believer for many years. He and his family are regular attendees at their local church and his wife is active with many of its programs. Tim is a good provider and a workaholic. Dependable to a fault, and like the rest of us, less than perfect. "At church," and for the most part, "at home" as well, he is a good example to his children and his fellow church members. However, away from home and the church, Tim is a bit different.

He does work hard. Plays hard too. Perhaps too hard. To unwind from a hectic day on the job, he regularly stops by a local bar with the guys. Kicks back a few drinks, flirts with the waitresses, plays one-up-man-ship with risqué jokes and stories about his own extra-marital escapades, drops expletives with no concern for how GOD's name is bantered about, and, just below the legal limit for driving under the influence, he heads for home.

At home he's a "model husband and father" except he is only there late in the evenings and most Sundays for church and rest. Saturdays are reserved for "Tim things" like golf, ballgames, and other guy things with his buddies from work and the bar. Affection for his wife is usually reserved for times when his own interests are involved. Tim has no time in his busy schedule for prayer and Bible Study, family growth time, mid-week church activities, or helping his neighbor with a car problem. But, if asked about his faith, Tim will quickly tell how he has that base covered: He is a "Christian" and not concerned about going to Hell.

God gets full credit for expressing His desire that "all" be saved. He has certainly made a provision for everyone to be included. Foxhole and deathbed conversions are just as real as the thief on the cross next to Jesus. The result is true salvation and then it's lights out. For the rest of us, we need to plunge our roots deep, seek some good water, grow in faith, and bear fruit of the Spirit as evidence of our true position in Christ.

It is necessary for believers to grow up in their faith. We must walk circumspectfully in our respective places while we prepare for the time when we will personally be in the presence of our Lord and Savior. That circumspect means we are to bear fruit. It is unacceptable for an individual to declare having a personal relationship with God through Christ and live unrepentantly in sin. Just as James, the brother of Christ said, "Show me your faith without deeds, and I will show you my faith by what I do," [48] it is the expectation of God Himself, that through the power of the Holy Spirit, a believer demonstrates their position in Christ by walking in the Spirit. Paul was most explicit about the fruit of the Spirit when he wrote ". . . the fruit of the Spirit is love, joy, peace, patience, kindness, goodness, faithfulness, gentleness and self-control. Against such things there is no law. Those who belong to Christ Jesus have crucified the sinful nature with its passions and desires. Since we live by the Spirit, let us keep in step with the Spirit." [49] Taken as written in the original language, the thought here could be rendered: The fruit of the Spirit is love, *demonstrated by* joy, peace, patience, etc. Rendered or un-rendered, God expects his children to bear fruit, and **love** is primary.

Positive, successful outreach and witnessing for Christ, demands our being committed to the "bearing of fruit" while we prepare to be with our Lord and Savior in the Kingdom of Heaven.

Selah

Put It in Your Heart Where Your Mind Can Find It

A special part of being a member of God's forever family is getting to remind yourself every day that you belong to Christ and there is nothing anyone can do that can remove that truth from your life. Jesus Christ Himself declared this fact when He was communicating with God the Father. Jesus said, "I have not lost one of those You gave me." [50] The Apostle John also recorded Jesus saying, "My sheep listen to My voice; I know them and they follow Me. I give them eternal life, and they shall never perish; no one can snatch them out of my hand. My Father, who has given them to Me is greater than all, no one can snatch them out of My Father's hand. I and the Father are One." [51] With that absolute truth, you can focus on putting your witnessing experience in your heart where your mind can find it. When you think about it, your feelings about your own personal salvation experience need to be available to your thought process when you are sharing the Gospel with someone. There are a few things you can do to organize your thoughts toward successful witnessing opportunities. The following "focus points" could be a starter group for you to build your thoughts around:

1. *Develop qualifying questions*—Questions fit for the occasion and tailored to "you and them." If you think your question might hinder the process, don't use it. Rethink it. Refine it, then present it.

2. *Know what you want to say*—Wait for the opening, then open your mouth and share the truth. Opportunity lost is opportunity wasted. Patience has its reward. Just remember, God has the first and the last word. (cf. Revelation 22.13). If He provides the opportunity He will have prepared their heart to receive the message. Count on it.

3. *Do not be shocked with "any" comeback*—Remember your position and more importantly, remember "whose" you are. Many with whom you want to share the truth don't want to hear it. They

will attempt to take your expressed interest in them and mock you. (cf. Lamentations 3.14). Their language and attitude may be objectionable. Your good example at this level will help, not hinder your effort.

4. *Stay on track*—Do not waltz around the subject. Focus or forget it, for now. You can come back to your point at a later time. Rambling on when you have been "knocked off-track" suggests an insecure position or attitude on your part. If you are easily rattled or distracted, work on it. Ol' what's his name can mess with your head only if you let him.

Know Where You Are

Showing yourself approved involves several elements. Another important part of being "approved," is knowing where you are when you share, or attempt to share the truth of the Gospel. It is always good if you know the environment you are in as well. A few points to consider in this regard, are:

1. *Be sensitive to time and place*—Bumping into a friend at work may provide an opportunity, but it may not be an appropriate time or place. Of course, this depends on the work place. The time may or may not be in conflict. If witnessing on the job presents any feeling of uneasiness for you or the one to whom you would be witnessing, then don't. Set a time and place away from the job. You will be more comfortable and so will your fellow worker. Remember, God has asked you to do the telling. Nowhere in His request is He agreeing or instructing you to compromise yourself or the message you are prepared to deliver.

Some time ago, during a structured break at the professional office where I worked, I became involved in sharing Christ with a fellow worker. The conversation was going well when the allotted time for the structured break expired. However, I got "wound-up" in presenting the Gospel and continued the discussion well beyond the time allocated for personal development.

After some time, a fellow worker rudely interrupted the conversation and suggested, "This is not the time and certainly not the place to be talking about religion. If you have to do that, do it on your own time, away from the office. No one wants to hear what you are discussing while they are trying to do their work. You guys should keep that kind of talk out of here."

Enthusiasm is a good thing. In this situation, enthusiasm brought compromise into play. It would have been better if I had been more sensitive to the time and deferred the conversation. It would have been very appropriate to acknowledge that the time allocated for the structured break was nearly over and suggest a continuation of the conversation at another time.

As it played out, the person to whom I was sharing was no longer open to that level of conversation at the office, and the rude co-worker went around gloating about having shut-down a religious meeting at the office. I was "branded" as a religious zealot and future opportunities to share the truth of Christ at the office were long in coming. Moral: Be sensitive.

2. *Be aware of situations*—You may knock at someone's door and discover that those to whom you would be witnessing are involved in a family situation that makes the moment awkward and less than convenient. Unless your relationship with them makes it comfortable for you to become involved, simply acknowledge the situation, request another time and excuse yourself. They will appreciate it and you will have demonstrated an attitude that is sensitive to their situation. They

will also remember that you did not force yourself into something that did not concern you.

3. *Be cognizant of circumstances*—Your friend has been involved in a relationship gone bad and the situation is affecting their life. You know that God wants only the best for His own and if they will come to Christ they could access ". . . the peace of God, which transcends all understanding, . . ." [52] Knowing a situation exists is a good thing. Being aware of the circumstance that produced it could enable you to be part of the solution. This is not to be considered a judgmental thing. If that's your bent, then your help is not needed. However, you may be a person who understands the circumstance and could help. You can approach the one in need and assist more if you are aware of the circumstance and have prepared yourself for the task at hand.

4. *Be available*—Doesn't make much of a difference how prepared we are, or how much we care about a specific person, their situation or circumstance, if we are not available. We are all busy. But busy is a relative term. We must not be so busy we cannot be available to share the truth with another person. Especially if that person has come to us. This doesn't imply that you should just drop whatever you are doing and get into the "sharing mood." It does mean that we should have an available attitude and when we have an opportunity or are called upon to become involved, we should be available to answer the call. Schedule a time with whomever it is that is involved. Honor the schedule and be available.

5. *Be flexible*—Flexible doesn't translate "pretzel." It means you can be less than rigid when it comes to your time management and/ or other areas of your life that are affected by your desire to be an effective witness for Christ. You are in charge of your schedule and when you need to be flexible you can. Schedules change. Circumstances alter situations. This is called life and you should become adapt and accommodating when the need arrives. Flexible also does not mean that

you are always the one that must do the accommodating. Circumstances and situations occur in your life as well. When you demonstrate an attitude of flexibility, it will come back to you at those times when you require a reciprocal application.

Know When to Quit

One thing all who are involved in witnessing should get a good grip on is knowing when to quit. You are not going to "talk" them in to it. In fact, pushing on with an argument or similar point of persuasion, when it is obvious you are not making any headway, could compromise yourself and anyone accompanying you in the witnessing effort. In Paul's letter to Titus, he wrote, ". . . avoid foolish controversies and genealogies and arguments and quarrels about the law, because these are unprofitable and useless. Warn a divisive person once, and then warn him a second time. After that, have nothing to do with him. You may be sure that such a man is warped and sinful; he is self-condemned." [53] You can tell when the conversation is going "off-point" and maybe even becoming contentious. You need to reserve the right, or the opportunity to talk again and back-off. You must always be prepared to walk away. But at the same time, you must be ready to "stand up for Jesus."

I remember a special time in my life when I was in another city with a brother in Christ. We were approached on a public sidewalk by an individual who was in obvious need of assistance. The individual was disheveled, unkempt and generally dirty in appearance. He was requesting money under the guise of trying to accumulate bus fare to his part of town. No strings attached, we offered a few dollars to the individual and were prepared to share the love of Christ with him. The man took the money immediately, but when Byron, my brother in Christ, attempted to share he began to verbally attack us. He accused us of being hypocrites, and people who thought we were better than someone like him. The tirade went to a lower level when the man began cursing and making a public scene. I knew this was not the time or the place to deal with the man and graciously asked the man to accept our apology for anything we might have said that offended him. We were attempting to take our leave when the man began defaming Christ.

I knew it was time to quit. I made it clear we were apologizing and were prepared to wait for another time. I was not going to compromise and allow ourselves to become part of a verbal street fight. However, the unkempt man was not yet through with his verbal abuse and with defaming words against Christ he became increasingly obnoxious.

Byron stepped closer to the defamer and firmly, without any physical overtures, gave the man a personal message from God. "You are dead in your sins. In the name of Jesus Christ, the Lord and Savior for all who believe, I rebuke you and your attitude toward God. You may be free to accuse us of things you feel are our shortcomings, but you may not bring insult against the Lord." Whether confused, dumbfounded or what, the man became speechless and walked away.

Later in the week, we came upon the same man who was again panhandling people on a sidewalk. He remembered us and came over to us. But instead of asking for money, he asked us how he could have the faith that we had demonstrated to him earlier. The truth was shared and the man asked Christ to save him and he became a born again Christian. Even though unverifiable, I believe this man is today, reaching out to down-trodden and desperate people who are living on the street.

Sample Questions—Not Stock Spiel

Witnessing is a challenge that requires preparation and a bit of dedication. A large library would be required to hold the multiple examples of witnessing and sample questions that could be posed to those to whom you are witnessing or attempting to share the Gospel. One thing that works against the process is "stock spiel" questions that have a rote feel and which are generally out-of-the-box type expressions.

As an approved witness you need to formulate your own questions and present them in your own words. It is definitely okay to research prepared tracts, articles and books. Many current-day and historical men and women of God have written excellent examples of questions and explanations for use in developing your own process for witnessing. The following questions and comments are neither all inclusive, nor meant to be taken as better examples for this part of outreach and evangelism. You are encouraged to look them over, add to them, modify them to your own taste and personality, and use them whenever and wherever you find them appropriate.

You can ask or present these questions as you determine applicability to a particular witnessing situation. The implied or suggested answers, along with a few of my own thoughts, are included with the questions to provide continuity.

Question:

- *If you were to die today: Would you be standing in the presence of God? Where would you be? Bound for Heaven, or Hell bound?*

This "set-up" question can be considered offensive or invasive and should not be presented "cold turkey" or in a flippant manner. The

Psalmist wrote, "Only God knows when our days on earth are done."[54] Everyone knows death is part of life, but most people just don't think about it. And, they usually don't want to talk about it. Especially if they are not born again. This question sets up a natural progression of discussion.

Broken down:

- **Would you be standing in the presence of God?**
  Only if you believe in Jesus[55]

Assuming they believe there is a God doesn't automatically give any assurance they will be standing before Him when death claims them. Non-believers will not stand before God until Judgment Day. The circumstance associated with their death is not the issue. Debate is also a situation you want to avoid when you are presenting questions to someone about their eternal security. Even though this question is simplistic, it is not simple.

- **Where would you be?**
  - **Bound for Heaven,?**
    A believer, absent from the body is present with the Lord[56]

The Word of God is the rule and guide for our faith. Paul telling the believers at Colosse the truth about the after death condition for those who believe in Christ, is one example among many. Telling someone who has not surrendered their life to Christ about this condition can become challenging. If Heaven is not in their future, there is only one other option available.

- **or Hell bound?**
  A non-believer, whose name is not written in the Lambs Book of Life, will be cast into the lake of fire.[57]

Just remember, you didn't say this, God did. You are simply the messenger. Going to Hell is a serious concern for anyone. Everyone with whom you have an opportunity to share knows about Hell. They may choose to ignore the truth or just not want to talk about it, but they do know about it. And, since it is not God's desire for anyone to go there, sharing the way to salvation is a privilege.

Question:

- *How would you answer God if He asked you: Why I should allow you into My Heaven? Is there a reason why you come to Me, now that your physical life is over?*

This is not a trick question. Believers confirm their faith with the answer. Non-believers are often times convicted in their spirits with this question and are brought to the place where they can accept Christ into their life. The door to Heaven isn't locked from God's side. But if it were, Christ is the key. (cf. Revelation 3.20). All anyone has to do is accept it and the key is theirs. There are those who believe, or hope, they have done enough good works and that God will welcome them into Heaven, or at worst, simply set them into a holding station while others petition God in their behalf. We all know that if this were God's plan, it would not have been necessary for Jesus Christ to be crucified.

Broken down:

- *Why I should allow you into My Heaven?*
  My Savior Jesus Christ has paid the price for me. He has washed away my sins with His blood. [58]

  <u>Anecdote</u>: A born again Christian was involved in a conversation with a "hard working, God fearing individual" who held the position that God put us on the

earth to be examples of what we are supposed to be doing in order to get to Heaven. This "hard working" individual was predisposed to the understanding that God would observe an individual's good works and compare them with those times when the individual had performed at a less-than-acceptable or in an unsatisfactory manner, and if the individual had performed enough or more "good works" than God required, then God would consider the individual acceptable and grant the individual a place in His Heaven.

The born again Christian asked if it were possible to know when one had done enough good work. The "hard working" individual said, "No one can ever know when they have done enough. Only God knows that. All we can do is work and hope God will accept our efforts." The born again Christian asked, "What happens if you haven't done enough?" To that, the "hard working" individual replied, "You go to Hell."

The dialog continued for some time, with the born again Christian listening to and presenting questions to the "hard working" individual along the way. At an appropriate time in the conversation the born again Christian asked, "Has anyone ever showed you from the Word of God that you can know for sure, right this very minute, whether or not God will accept you into His Heaven?" (*I don't believe so.*) "May I share this truth with you now?" (*Yes.*) The born again Christian shared the Gospel with the "hard working" individual and another soul was saved by the blood of Jesus. The "hard working" individual accepted the truth. Halleluiah!

- *Is there a reason why you come to Me, now that your physical life is over?*
  So that I can warn others before it's too late for them to choose rightly [59]

The Bible is pretty straight forward on this issue. You didn't believe while you were physically on the earth. Those with whom you would now share the truth wouldn't believe you either. They have the same opportunity as you and have not accepted the truth. Your telling them, even if you could, would not change anything.

Question:

- *Do you have eternal security?*
  Yes / No. Only in Christ [60]

The answer is short: Yes or no. If they have eternal security it must be based on something. Christ is the only correct answer. If they do not, then you have the opening you are looking for to present a better option.

Question:

- *What does eternal life mean—is it real?*
  To be with God forever and ever and yes, it is absolutely real [61]

The Word of God specifically tells us we know that we are known to God before we are born. (cf. Jeremiah 1.5). And, when born we take a physical position in an eternal program. So, eternity is a before, during and after thing in which everyone has a place. Eternal life is forever. Even when our physical existence ceases, we continue on with our eternal journey. The concept can be difficult to grasp, but it is real. God has presented His plan for our eternal existence and He wants us to spend it with Him.

Question:

- **How can anyone know they have eternal life?**
  Confess and believe [62]

Confession is certainly good for the soul, but this question deals with eternal life. We can know with certainty that our eternal home is with the Lord if we confess and believe. (cf. 1 John 5.13). The calming effect of this truth can only be shared if we have it ourselves. With this wonderful truth we can begin to enjoy our eternal life with God, not fear eternal life separated from Him.

Question:

- **What do you believe?**
  It's a mystery [63]

Even if they say they don't believe in anyone or anything, they do. They just deny it because they do not want to be seen as counting on anyone or anything but themselves. Circumstances or situations in their life may have warped their thinking and God is just not someone or something they want to acknowledge. The Bible tells us only a fool would say there is no God. (cf. Psalm 14.1). With certainty, God is a mystery to those who do not believe. But, if someone denies God they are being foolish or at best, insincere. If, and it won't be uncommon, some claim a belief in a system or a person (real, or just an idea), you will have more than an opportunity to share the truth, you may also have the privilege of defending your faith.

Question:

- **How do you know it is true?**
  God said it and that settles it. [64]

Believers and even some non-believers understand that there is nothing impossible with God. With that said, there must also be a firm understanding, that with everything God can do, there is one thing He cannot do: Lie. From the beginning until and through all eternity future, God cannot lie. What He has said; what He will say is absolute truth. We can choose to believe and accept, but when God speaks to an issue that settles it. Agreeing or disagreeing with God is on us. Better to agree.

Question:

- *Is faith real or abstract?*
  Absolutely real[65]

We know that God is real. We know that our faith in Jesus is real. And, because of our faith, we have eternal security. But there are those who have no understanding or comprehension of faith. They do not know what it means to place their faith in someone (something) they cannot see. There are several examples of practical faith all around us. Airplanes and elevators are common to our time. Getting on or into one is a statement of faith, albeit silent and without fanfare. You have "faith" in the equipment. You exercise that level of faith when you step onto a plane or into an elevator. The skeptic will say, "Yes, but I know the plane will fly and that the elevator will operate." How do you know? You cannot see the pilot or observe the sophisticated apparatus that runs the elevator. Do you have faith they will perform and that you will arrive safely at your destination? Is your faith real? Is it abstract? Yes to the real, and no to the abstract. Skeptic again, "Yes, but I can see them." Okay, the earth rotates around the sun every year. You can see it with the sunrise and sunset, but you cannot feel it. The moon rotates around the earth. You can see it but you cannot feel it. Yet, they affect your life in very dramatic ways. Do you have faith that these events will continue? Is that faith real? Is it abstract? Again, yes and no . . . . Just a thought.

As for "saving faith," Scripture is specific, direct and very clear: You must believe and accept what the Lord did in your behalf on faith. Faith in Jesus Christ alone, by whose grace we are saved. You cannot smell it or taste it, but unlike practical faith, you most certainly can feel it.

Question:

- ***What is keeping you from believing?***
  Any excuse will do[66]

As foolish as it may sound or seem, if a person doesn't want to accept eternal security, any excuse will become plausible to them.

> Anecdote: During a witnessing encounter, a believer shared the Gospel with a man named Bill, and presented a closing question which asked if there was any reason to not accept God's offer of an eternal relationship with Him. Bill's answer was typical of those often presented by non-believers. "Well, I've given this God idea some thought and I'm just not ready." The believer shared from Scripture that now was the appointed time. (cf. 2 Corinthians 6.2). To which Bill responded, "What you say makes sense, but I know I wouldn't be able to be the type of person God wants me to be right now, so I'm gonna give it some more time. Besides, I'm not going to die today. There's lots of time to check this out."
>
> The news that evening carried a report of a car accident which resulted in the death of the driver. It was a man named Bill. Not necessarily that same Bill, but . . .

Question:

- *Are you everything God wants you to be?*
  Work in progress[67]

We are all "works in progress." (cf. Philippians 1.6). God gave us all an example to follow: Himself, through the Son of God, Jesus Christ. Only Christ is capable of living an earthly life without the compromise of sin. The only pre-requisite for us is accepting Christ and then, since we are less than Christ, we must work "out of our salvation" to be the person God wants us to be while we are on the earth.

Question:

- *Have you ever thought about: Life after death? What is Hell like? What is life all about? Heaven as a real forever place? The Bible being more than a book?*

Broken Down:

- *Life after death?*
  Yes / No[68]

Yes is most always the answer. Anyone past the age of twelve has thought about death. As the life experience continues everyone becomes aware of at least the possibility of life after death. To the believer, death is only a doorway to pass through to a new and better life with God. To the non-believer, death is just the end. To those who hold to a false, or non-Christ faith, death can be viewed without fear, but there is no certainty as to what the after death life will be. With God, there should be no fear of death. (cf. Hosea 13.14). We can share this truth as well.

- **What is Hell like?**
  Torment [69]

Regardless of what anyone calls it, or when anyone goes there, Hell is a horrible and most uncomfortable place. But, whatever, whenever or wherever you believe Hell is, it should be understood that Hell, or Hades, is not the final destination for the lost. (cf. 2 Peter 2.4). During His earthly existence, Christ referred to Hell as that place where the lost are confined until the White Throne Judgment, when those that are there will be brought out and cast into the Lake of Fire, where the lost are doomed to spend eternity.

- **What is life all about?**
  Serving God [70]

Life is knowing who we are in Christ. Life is also dispensational. In our physical life today, in this time before the return of the Lord, we are involved with choosing our eternal destiny. It is that period where we are responsible for how we live and honor the Creator. As Believers, our life after physical death will be involved with worshiping and loving the Savior, in preparation for His return and the "catching away" of all the believers alive on the earth at that moment. Our life then will be involved with living and reigning with the Lord until the White Throne Judgment. Beyond that we will continue with the Lord forever. Without Christ there is no life, only death and the penalty associated with it.

- **Heaven as a real forever place?**
  God has always "been" [71]

God's plan from creation is to have those who believe in Him and accept His will for their life, to be with Him forever. Heaven is the eternal destination for all believers. God has always been and His place has always been Heaven. When His plan is completed, all who believe will be with Him in a new Heaven.

- **The Bible being more than a book?**
  Infallible Word of God[72]

Evidence supporting the validity of Scripture is overwhelming. Scoffers can only repeat what they have read or heard from skeptics. No serious evaluation of the historic manuscripts has taken anything away from the fact that God's Word has been meticulously examined and preserved for us. Faithful translations are available that enable us to read and understand the truth and to know without doubt that Christ is the main focus of the Bible.

Question:

- **How many "religions" are there? Which ones are right? Is there a "true" religion?**

If personal interpretations are considered, along with all known isms and cults, the number of "religions" can easily be estimated to be in the thousands. Jesus reminded all His followers about the pit-falls associated with trying to be religious. (cf. Matthew 5.20). Keeping the law is impossible. Adhering to a program of mantras and such is even more impossible. God is not asking anyone to become religious. He is asking that all who want to be with Him and enjoy His presence eternally, simply by faith, accept His provision: Jesus Christ.

Broken Down:

- **Which ones are right?**
  None[73]

Arguing about religion can occupy as well as waste a lot of your time. Religious dogma is not what God has in mind when He encourages us to not forsake the coming together as believers for the purpose of worship and praise. Religion has a way of getting in the way when it comes to knowing God and who you are in His forever family. Sometimes satisfying a preconceived idea about what you believe someone else believes can result in some very serious negative feelings and produce even more confusion. There is one true God and one way to access a personal relationship with Him: Jesus. No religion provides that opportunity. Labels may help us focus our thoughts and actions toward God centered activities, but they cannot change our hearts. No religion is capable of saving anyone. We need to know why we agree or disagree with whomever and/or whichever system or religious philosophy. With that confirmation in our minds and hearts we can reach out to those with whom we are witnessing and, instead of being intimidated, we can challenge the misrepresentations by those who hide in the dogma of some religious program.

- **Is there a "true" religion?**
  No[74]

Religion is man's idea. And, like most "man centered" activities, religion can be, and in many aspects has been, manipulated to exalt an individual or dogma ordained by man. There are plenty of religions that are true to their own understandings and interpretations of their own concept of faith. But, there are no "true" religions. And, even more specifically, there is no "this is it" religion. The world is always in conflict because of over-zealous followers of religious pundits. We need and should seek the encouragement of like minded people who are following Biblical concepts of/for a church. God has ordained the Church and wants believers to be part of something that brings them together around sound Biblical precepts. God's Word is true and should be acknowledged religiously. Through the principals of God's Word our faith is nourished and our hearts, our true personalities, are guided to the truth of Jesus Christ. With this truth flowing in our life, we can be proper examples to those who need to know the truth.

Question:

- ***Why was Jesus required to die?***
  Only one way [75]

God does not need to prove anything to anyone. He is All and in all and He knew before creating anyone or anything that there would be a void in the process. And, since He knows the ending, he knew what would be required of His creation to be part of His forever family. Ol' what's his name was busy early and God allowed it. For God's creation to become what God intends it to be, God would intervene in the affairs of man and provide a way for any and all who would or will believe, to claim and enjoy an eternal relationship with Him. God chose a specific time in the process to demonstrate His commitment to His own creation. Without abandoning His position as Supreme Being, He took upon Himself the form of man. He was physically born, grew into and acquired the stature of an adult and walked among His creation as the man Jesus Christ. He openly shared the truth with those around Him, and in accordance with His plan, laid down His life as a sacrifice for those He loves. Jesus had to die a physical death, so that through His own death and resurrection He would provide a way for all mankind to fill the void that separates man from God. Through the death of His Son, Jesus Christ, God the Father took upon Himself the deficiencies of all mankind, and with Christ's resurrection, He claimed the souls of all who had died in faith and took them with Him to Heaven.

You can play around with this fact until your brain gives out, but the truth will always be there: God is not willing[*] that any should

---

[*] In this instance "willing" in the Greek is *boulemai,* which means "by force of will—making it happen."

perish. [76] Heaven will be occupied by those who will. The Lake of Fire will claim all those who will not.

Statement:

- *This list could go on and on . . .*

But here is one opener, or question, that will offend no one but the Devil, put the person at ease, give you a place to go with your conversation, move or start the topic at the right place, and is very comfortable for you:

- *How are you and the Lord getting along these days?*

You can take their answer right where you need to go; the Bible. You've opened the door. Now you need to walk through it.

Questions

Very common questions often times surfaces when you are attempting to share the Gospel with non-believers, or even with those who profess to believe but just aren't sure about:

Who is this Jesus?

Scripture is a very appropriate place to direct your response to this question.

And He shall be called: (f)

Advocate, Shiloh, The Resurrection and The Life, Shepherd and Bishop of Souls, Judge, Master, Lord of Lords, Rock, Man of Sorrows, Savior, Head of the Church, Faithful and True Witness, Servant, High Priest, Living Water, Bread of Life, Rose of Sharon, Messiah [77], Alpha and Omega, True Vine, Teacher, Holy One, I Am, Mediator, The Beloved, Good Shepherd, Branch, Light of the World, Son of God, The Almighty, Carpenter, Image of the Invisible God, The Door, The Word, Bridegroom, Chief Cornerstone, Redeemer, Author and Finisher of Our Faith, Everlasting Father, Lamb of God, King of Kings, Lion of the Tribe of Judah, Anchor, Prophet, Only Begotten Son, Wonderful Counselor, Immanuel, Son of Man, Dayspring, The Amen, King of the Jews, Bright Morning Star, Prince of Peace, The Way The Truth and The Life, **Jesus Christ.**

CHAPTER SIX

MAKE CHRIST THE TOPIC

Often a Difficult Thing to Do
A Natural Thing to Do
Christ Probably Had/Has Something to Say About It
Let the Situation/Individual Set the Tone
Your Christianity Should Not Be a Secret
Opportunities to Make Christ the Topic
How do you do it?

Questions

Outreach, witnessing and evangelism involve communicating a truth that is commonly considered a foreign topic by many of those with whom you wish to share. It is a rare, if not a non-existent occasion, when someone in your path introduces a "Christ inquiry." Most normally you will have to steer the conversation toward spiritual things in order to make Christ the topic. Whatever the situation, it remains a believer's responsibility to make good use of an opportunity to witness. God is completely aware of the situation. You need to trust Him while you are moving around in the areas of opportunity.

Often a Difficult Thing to Do

There are those who take to witnessing as if it were the most natural thing to do. Others though, have some reservations when it comes to being involved in outreach or evangelistic activities. For these folks, it is often a difficult thing to do. Perhaps the following could shed some light on this topic. A few "Why" questions will set the tone. And, providing a "Reason" could set-up a general discussion.

Why	Reason
Don't know how	**Never done it before**

The obvious answer for this potential dilemma is to get into the "doing side" of outreach. Think of, or consider an individual you know who is involved in the ministry of evangelism. That person had an initial experience in witnessing. With that event in their rear view mirror, an evangelistic ministry was launched. Remember the Apostle Paul. He wrote in his letter to the believers at Philippi, "I can do everything through him who gives me strength." [1] Doesn't mean you should quit your day job, but it does underscore the fact that the doing of it makes the doing of it more comfortable and removes the syndrome of "I've never done this before." Get with someone who is doing it. You will be encouraged and become comfortable with your experience. It is generally understood that once you have done something it becomes easier to repeat the effort. Not doing something becomes all too easy as well. Accept the challenge and prepare yourself for the rewards that follow. The Apostle Paul, in his first letter to the Corinthians said, "For no one can lay any foundation other than the one already laid, which is Jesus Christ. If any man builds on this foundation using gold, silver, costly stones, wood, hay or straw, his work will be shown for what it is, because the Day[*] will bring it to light. It will be revealed with fire, and the fire will test the quality of each man's work. If what he has built survives, he will receive his reward. If it is burned up, he will suffer loss; he himself will be saved, but only as one escaping through the flames." [2]

Warren Doud, in Grace Notes wrote, "There is a reward for witnessing. Rewards in Heaven are an extension of edification; the only things that are rewarded in Heaven are what is done on the basis of Grace. Thus, every reward in Heaven is an eternal memorial to the grace of God. Grace means that rewards do not reflect any personal glory or merit. It is the Lord who enables us to labor for Him and who provides the divine production in the life (gold, silver, and precious stones)." [a]

Why   Reason

Would, but I just can't   I'm afraid to do it

---

[*]   Refers to the prophesied Day of the Lord (Christ's return). A day had also been prophesied for the destruction of Jerusalem, which occurred in 70 AD (cf: Daniel 9.26) when Rome conquered the nation of Israel and totally destroyed Herod's Temple.

Fear visits everyone. How you deal with it, particularly in the arena of outreach, witnessing and evangelism, is the main focus of this question.

Meeting with strangers, even family members for that matter, and attempting to introduce them to the truth of Jesus Christ is sometimes a fearful undertaking. Fear is a normal emotion, but we are to remember that God did not give us a spirit of fear. Remember the words of Paul in his second letter to Timothy, "For God did not give us a spirit of timidity, but a spirit of power, of love and of self-discipline." [3] If you are operating as a "lone ranger" it is possible for you to be out there without prayer cover and come across someone who becomes so disturbed or enraged by your intrusion that you become "fearful" for your own position, or maybe your own safety.

Committing yourself to the opportunity before it occurs and asking God to direct the right person to you should put you at ease with yourself and any potential witnessing encounter. And, with prayer support from those in your local body of believers, you will be continually encouraged when and if you become involved in sharing the truth of Christ with an unbeliever.

<u>Why</u>	<u>Reason</u>
Easier said than done	**Harder than it looks**

This is an element of perception. If you think it is hard or difficult, you can easily convince yourself that it is. Many believers who should be involved in outreach have taken the "laid back" approach to witnessing. They sit on their hands, so to speak, because they feel the work of evangelism will consume too much of their time and become an arduous undertaking that is too demanding. They don't feel comfortable in their own position in Christ. They have convinced themselves that they cannot do the work. When you take this position it is just easier to do nothing. Then it doesn't matter if the work is hard or not.

Why	Reason
Sometimes we look for an excuse	**(WY • ALFAE • AE • WD)**

When you ~ are looking for an excuse ~ any excuse ~ will do (WY • ALFAE • AE • WD). We are all guilty of looking for an excuse to, or not to do something. Witnessing usually falls into the "not to do" category. "I would, but I have a cuticle problem on one of my fingers." Ridiculous? Certainly. But you get the idea. We are presented with an opportunity to witness and for whatever reason, we opt out. After a while, it becomes the normal program of response to just use an excuse. "I wanted to be involved, but that hangnail . . ." Ol' what's his name will present any excuse to keep us out of the fray. God has provided all we need to be ambassadors for the truth. He has given us Christ: The real excuse for us to use when we encounter an opportunity to share our faith.

A Natural Thing to Do

In reality, witnessing is just a natural thing to do. You can talk with others about most anything, so seize the moment and go for it. Remember, it's a natural thing to do.

As a simple illustration, let's say you are talking with a good friend or perhaps a business associate named "Tom." Talking with him should provide multiple opportunities to talk about matters of faith. With a little patience you may come to the moment where sharing just becomes natural. Remember, rote is not the objective. In your own style and in your own words, like introducing a friend, you could say, "Tom, I'd like to introduce you to my best friend." (Christ is your best friend—isn't he?). Once you have introduced Christ into the conversation, Christ just flows out from you.

Moving forward you might want to say something like, "Tom, Jesus is such a real part of my life." Then you can confirm your relationship with Christ by saying something like, "Tom, I don't know what I would do without Jesus."

Tom most assuredly will have something to say in response to your expression of faith. Since Christ likeness is an enablement, you can respond with, "Like the Bible says Tom, 'I can do all things . . .'[4] When I know it's what God wants, I can do it. My faith in Him produces a confidence I never knew before I let Christ have control of my life."

Christ Probably Had/Has Something to Say About It

If we claim Christ's position as ours, up front, at the beginning of an encounter, there is no problem staying with the process. No matter what we come up against, we can know with confidence that we have the truth. If you encounter **bad language**: God says, "We are not to take His name in vain"[5] He also says, "Let no corrupt communication come out of your mouth"[6]

> Anecdote: It may have been yesterday. It may be today. It could be tomorrow. But, at some point you had or will have an opportunity to deal with an individual who is using inappropriate language. You can calmly say something that puts that person on notice. If that is not something you can do, try this: Simply raise your hand (arm bent at the elbow, palm toward you, non-

threatening) and cover the offender's line of sight to you. Wherever the offender moves, move your hand to cover the line of sight. When you are asked what it is you are doing, you can quite matter-of-factly let the offender know you consider the language offensive. And, if asked to explain your position, it will be easy to respond with God's position on the matter. Another "shut-down" is to simply ask the name of the offender's father. Then ask the offender if it would be appropriate to use that name as part of a curse word. Example: The offender's father's name happens to be Frank. Would it be appropriate to ask Frank to damn something, or to refer to someone or something as a "Frank-damned" someone or something? Again, the offender will quickly get the point.

Your position will be understood and the "potty-mouth" will stop spewing the offensive language, at least for the moment. If not, then simply turn your back on it and the offender and walk away. And, if that is not possible at the time, just turning away and disengaging yourself from the conversation is the thing to do. This can be applied to "smut-talkers" as well. Anyone observing your actions, including the offender, will get your point.

Everyone can, and probably will, have a bad day. Perhaps more than a few. But a **bad attitude** is cultivated. It may come on gradually, but a bad attitude is like the farmer getting a crop in the ground, you have to work at it. And after all, you reap what you have sown. Feeling great or feeling bad and experiencing sorrow is part of life. These are driven by situation and circumstance. A bad attitude is a choice. We need to remember that God says, "Get rid of all bitterness, rage and anger, brawling and slander, along with every form of malice."[7] And, as the Apostle Paul wrote in his letter to the Philippians, ". . . whatever is true, whatever is noble, whatever is right, whatever is pure, whatever is lovely, whatever is admirable—if anything is excellent or praiseworthy—think about such things." [8] This is the field that needs to be cultivated. The crop harvested from this effort will infuse us with a proper attitude and enable us to be more effective as representatives of Christ.

Decisions are also part of life's experience. We make them regularly and then live with the consequences. But *poor moral judgment* is not what God expects from the family of believers. Even with the certainty of our own lack of perfection we can share what we know to be true when we are witnessing for Christ. As an encouragement to completed Jews, the Apostle Peter, in his first general epistle wrote, "Dear friends, I urge you, as aliens and strangers in the world, to abstain from sinful desires, which war against your soul." [9] Even the earliest Christians had to war with the desires of the flesh and the immorality of that day. One of the first written instructions from God to His chosen people, and subsequently to the entire world, was etched in stone: "You shall not covet your neighbor's house. You shall not covet your neighbor's wife, or his manservant or maidservant, his ox or donkey, or anything that belongs to your neighbor." [10] This commandment has been around for quite a long time. But, there are plenty of God's people who cannot keep their minds or their hands off what does not belong to them. Immorality is bred in this environment and the result is poor moral judgment. It would be best if everyone could just accept God at His Word and just not covet another's anything. Part of witnessing is accepting our individual responsibility to walk circumspectly before unbelievers.

Ethics, or perhaps better put, the lack of ethics breeds bad attitudes, hate, discontentment and disrespect for authority. Neighbors cheat on neighbors; professionals scheme and connive against other professionals; church members talk behind the backs of other church members; and those whom you trust the most find ways to fit their aspirations in ahead of yours. Many of those you encounter as a witness for Christ have been used, misused and abused by the program or process to which they had committed themselves. They are hurt and disillusioned and not interested in hearing about how great it is to be a Christian.

Careful is an underused approach when it comes to ministering to those who need to hear the truth but have a negative feeling about all things associated with organized religion because they have been on the receiving end of some malicious gossip or other type of ethical breech. The writer of Proverbs presented God's thought on man's concept of right and wrong when he wrote, "There is a way that seems right to a man, but in the end it leads to death." [11] Putting that understanding into a witnessing opportunity may take some doing, but you can temper it with the words of the Apostle Matthew who wrote in his Gospel, ". . . every good tree bears good fruit, but a bad tree bears bad fruit." [12]

When it comes to ethics, a person with an unethical attitude toward others would be considered a bad tree and the bearer of bad fruit. Make certain you are not compromised when you approach someone in the name of Jesus. We always need to be aware of "whose" we are.

Considered a blessing, *money* can also be a curse. Often referred to as "filthy lucre," money captures the minds and hearts of many. Regardless of its denomination: Dollars, Rubles, Yen, Pésos, Guilders, Marks, Francs, Sheqels, Pounds, or whatever, money does represent a local and international economy. Money is also the measure often used to gauge the success of businesses and, whether rightly or wrongly, it is used to measure individuals as well. Those who have money do not appear overly concerned about those who do not. And, those who do not have money are prone to be envious of those who do. Through the Apostle Paul, in his first letter to Timothy, God says, "For the love of money is a root of all kinds of evil. Some people eager for money, have wandered from the faith and pierced themselves with many griefs." [13] Greed and conniving are the results. And, we should remember that God also says, "Each one should use whatever gift he has received to serve others, faithfully administering God's grace in its various forms." [14] We are to be proper stewards of what God has given us.

Witnessing, outreach and evangelism involves many things, but one, if not the most essential component is *love*. Not romantic love, but that love we reserve for and toward others with and for whom we care. And since we care for the lost, we should demonstrate love toward them. In John's Gospel, he recorded the words of Christ, who said, "This is my command: Love each other." [15] Sharing Christ is something we do with love. We are to love one another. Especially believers.

Love replaces any attitude of malice we might have toward another person. In Paul's letter to the Romans, he wrote, "Love must be sincere. Hate what is evil; cling to what is good. Be devoted to one another in brotherly love. Honor one another above yourselves." [16]

When you are dealing with someone who demonstrates a less than kind reception toward your attempts to share the truth of Christ, remember what Paul wrote to the believers at Corinth. "Love is patient, love is kind. It does not envy, it does not boast, it is not proud. It is not rude, it is not self-seeking, it is not easily angered, it keeps no record of wrongs. Love does not delight in evil but rejoices with the truth. It always protects, always trusts, always hopes, always perseveres." [17] Think about it. If you show love toward another person the reward is already yours. Give it a chance to work its wonder with one who is hardened by life.

There is wisdom associated with the old adage "you catch more flies with honey than you do with vinegar." We may not understand the circumstance or situation another person may be experiencing, but we can show God's love to that person. We can share our faith. Even our hope. But, just as Paul included in his letter to the Corinthians, ". . . the greatest of these is love." [18]

We are all guilty of having and even sharing *bad thoughts*. This is another area that gets involved with witnessing, outreach and evangelism. Admonishing the believers at Rome, the Apostle Paul wrote, "For by the grace given me I say to every one of you: Do not think of yourself more highly than you ought, but rather think of yourself with sober judgment, in accordance with the measure of faith God has given you." [19] Conversely, we should not think less of ourselves than we should either. That could, and often does result in our thinking ill of ourselves which can evolve into our developing bad thoughts toward others. We should always remember that God is not impressed by our bad thought life.

Along with bad language, bad attitudes, poor moral judgments, inappropriate ethics, money (i.e. filthy lucre), love of/for others, and bad thoughts, there is always all of those *other things*. Whatever they might be, God has provided an understanding that all believers should grasp: The writer of Ecclesiastes wrote, "What has been will be again, what has been done will be done again; there is nothing new under the sun." [20] God made all things perfect from the beginning. Things known and unknown to/by the created are not unknown to the Creator. Given this thought from God, we must understand that anything apart from God is meaningless. Without God it won't last and is insignificant. Once we have come to the place where we know without a doubt that we are born again into God's forever family, we need to seek God's will for whatever it is we are to be about. Witnessing, outreach and evangelism represent a very significant part of a Believer's life. Running with this understanding is the responsibility for those who believe to speak up. As David wrote in the Book of Psalms, "Let the redeemed of the Lord say this—those he redeemed from the hand of the foe." [21] If you are under conviction about something that is going on around you, speak up. God will honor your commitment. Paul reminded the believers at Corinth in his first letter to them, that "God, who has called you into fellowship with his Son Jesus Christ our Lord, is faithful." [22] Basically this means you can count on God.

Let the Situation/Individual Set the Tone

Having concern for the lost is a prerequisite for any outreach or witnessing effort. And, while being prepared to share the truth is a very important part of the process, knowing when to share is also an essential element. Being sensitive to and aware of situations and/or individual positions which affect those with whom we are wanting to or attempting to share is primary. The Apostle Peter, in his first general epistle wrote, ". . . live in harmony with one another; be sympathetic, love as brothers, be compassionate and humble." [23] Some guidelines in this area may be helpful. Aside from Christ, no one individual or ministry has all the answers. However, the following "rules of engagement" may be of assistance:

Don't force the subject

If you invade someone's privacy or speak out of turn, you will compromise the moment and lose whatever edge you might have gained by waiting for an invitation. David, the Psalmist, wrote, "Wait for the Lord; be strong and take heart and wait for the Lord." [24] There is no need, impending or otherwise, that compels us to jump into a Gospel presentation just because we are present when a situation is observed. You will be respected and more readily accepted if you don't force your way into a conversation or circumstance.

Respond "as a matter of truth"

God has given you the opportunity to speak for Him. What you say is as important, if not more so, than how you say it. God's Word is truth. The writer of Hebrews put it this way: "For the word of God is living and active. Sharper than any double-edged sword, it penetrates even to dividing soul and spirit, joints and marrow; it judges the thoughts and attitudes of the heart." [25] Speak the truth to whatever it is you are addressing. Quote Scripture if it fits into the conversation. If not, speak what you know to be true from your heart, based on the Word of God.

Be yourself

Don't try to respond or act the way you think someone else might. You are you. If what you say means anything to whomever it is, then your follow-up will have to be part of you as well. If you are out of character in your witnessing, you will not be taken seriously. Especially by someone you already know.

> Anecdote: A well-known Southern based evangelist with a distinct presentation of the truth, made a lasting and dynamic impression on a believer who felt called to be a witness for Christ in every area of his life. This believer became determined to share the Gospel with anyone at any time and took the evangelist's style as a method. All good except the evangelist's style was from a different culture than that represented by the enthusiastic believer. When presented with an opportunity to share, the believer turned on or tuned-in to the evangelist's style. Result: More attention was paid to the mannerism than to the message.

A person from the South won't draw undo or unnatural attention to the manner and mannerism of speech when speaking to another person in or from the South. Similar understanding could be applied to any area of the Country. A person born and raised in the Northeast will certainly come to some ridicule if every time a conversation moves toward a Gospel presentation, the person making the presentation takes on another personality or characteristic of speech. Some may even reject the truth on the basis that if becoming a Christian makes you talk like that, forget it.

If you are from the South and in another area of the Country, being yourself is expected. If you are from the Northeast and attempt to present yourself in an unnatural way, you will not be taken seriously. Be yourself. God accepted you and will accept others from all cultures and walks of life. Those with whom you wish to share will more readily accept you and the message if you don't use an unnatural approach.

Be Compassionate

Often found missing in witnessing and outreach is the deliberate and honest demonstration of compassion. We should follow the example of Jesus Himself and be compassionate toward those to whom we are sharing the truth of Christ. The Apostle Matthew provided such an example when he wrote in his gospel, "Jesus went through all the towns and villages, teaching in their synagogues, preaching the good news of the kingdom and healing every disease and sickness. When he saw the crowds, he had compassion on them, because they were harassed and helpless, like sheep without a shepherd." [26]

Delivered in a sermon titled *The Compassion of Jesus*, C. H. Spurgeon said, "I suppose that when our Saviour looked upon certain sights, those who watched him closely perceived that his internal agitation was very great, his emotions were very deep, and then his face betrayed it, his eyes gushed like founts with tears, and you saw that his big heart was ready to burst with pity for the sorrow upon which his eyes were gazing. He was moved with compassion. His whole nature was agitated with commiseration for the sufferers before him." [(b)].

Anecdote: Richard, a genuine man of God and brother in Christ, works for a local government agency as a financial planner and counselor. He visits with elderly clients in their homes to undertake financial assessments of the charges for their care and benefits and to evaluate whether or not their income could be increased by applying for and receiving various governmental benefits. Richard has a very pleasant manner and personality, which he has dedicated to the Lord, and often, at the end of a fiscal assessment a client will comment as to what a nice person he is. To which, Richard replies, "Well, to tell you the truth, this is not my real job." The client, along with other family members, if present, is intrigued at this point and usually wants to know what it is Richard considers his real job to be. With that door opened, Richard replies, "I am a Church Minister" and proceeds to tell them what he does, which includes sharing the "Good News" about Jesus Christ. This has lead, on a number of occasions, to Richard praying a prayer of faith with those present.

Many of his clients are suffering with some type of illness or disease, and Richard feels great compassion for them, wanting them to know that in their great need Jesus Christ has come to save and seek the lost. This type of witnessing allows Richard to utilize his natural God directed personality, to demonstrate true compassion through the power of the Holy Spirit for the honor and glory of Jesus Christ.

When a person walks with God, with a pure heart and clean hands, it allows the Holy Spirit to open doors for that person to share the Gospel. This Gospel is not always the spoken word, but is the very presence of Jesus Christ that is being presented when that person comes in contact with another person's life. In one home where Richard was serving a client, not a word was spoken about Jesus Christ, but as Richard was about to leave the house, the client, an elderly man with whom Richard had been dealing, suddenly grabbed Richard's hand and said, "Please pray for me. I can see a light shining from your life and I want to know that light." Richard not only prayed for the man, but also ministered the Gospel of Jesus Christ to him and others that were present.

Compassion, especially toward lost and unregenerated sinners, is an important part in allowing a particular situation or individual to establish the tone for a witnessing encounter. In his first general epistle, the Apostle Peter reaffirmed this position for Christians when he wrote, "Finally, all of you, live in harmony with one another; be sympathetic, love as brothers, be compassionate and humble." [27] And, like a positive attitude, compassion must be cultivated in your own life.

Remember your place

You are not a martyr. It is Christ who offends, not you. The Apostle Matthew addressed this situation in his gospel when he quoted Christ, who said, "Blessed are you when people insult you, persecute you and falsely say all kinds of evil against you because of Me. Rejoice and be glad, because great is your reward in Heaven, for in the same way they persecuted the prophets who were before you." [28] All Christ asks you to do is tell them. You can make yourself available for future discussion or whatever, but when you are making a first or one time statement, you are the messenger, not the message. The only way you can personally offend someone is for you to become offensive.

Don't overreact

When your involvement is rejected or ridiculed, don't become defensive. Don't attempt to put them in their place with a few well-chosen and rehearsed "righteous words of indignation." If you have a situation where walking away is the best action to take, take it. Your faith is not in question. But you can demonstrate a high level of self control and earn the privilege of talking with them again.

Your Christianity Should Not Be a Secret

A well-known song from adult and children ministries alike makes the following statement: "If you are saved and you know it, then your life will surely show it." The author takes exception to the word "will" in the lyrics of this song and suggests a more applicable word would be "should." Not everyone who is saved has the freedom to openly express their personal relationship with Jesus Christ, (those who live in communities where no tolerance is given for any God-concept other than the mandated system espoused by misguided, and/or worse, tyrannical leaders). But everyone who is saved should be demonstrating with their life's actions that they are different from those who are lost.

John MacArthur wrote in The Gospel According to Jesus, "Faith obeys. Unbelief rebels. The fruit of one's life reveals whether that person is a believer or an unbeliever. There is no middle ground (. . . *this is not to deny the obvious truth that Christians can and do fall into sin. But even in the case of a sinning believer, the Spirit will operate by producing conviction, hatred for his sin, and some kind of desire for obedience. The idea that a true believer can continue in unbroken disobedience from the moment of conversion, without ever producing any righteous fruit whatsoever, is foreign to Scripture*). Merely knowing and affirming facts apart from obedience to the truth is not believing in the biblical sense. Those who cling to the memory of a one-time decision of 'faith' but lack any evidence that faith has continued to operate in their lives had better heed the clear and solemn warning of Scripture. (cf. John 3.36)" [b]

We all know believers, and if we don't it will not be difficult to imagine, those who are open and aggressive with their Christian exuberance on Sunday and then demonstrate their general *laissez faire* attitude about Christ during the rest of the week, or anytime they are away from a Christian forum. This probably involves some personal evaluation as well, but, if your Christianity is a secret, you need to:

Open up

Allow God to be seen in your life. Before you were saved you had no hope of eternal security. With the complete understanding that today is the first day of the rest of your life, you can rejoice in knowing that even if today were to be your last day on earth, you have been saved forever. Somehow, when reflecting on this personal truth for your life, it just seems right for a gleam to be in your eye and a smile in residence on your face. If nothing else, it will probably result in those around you asking, or at least wondering, what is it that you have, that they don't. This is not a "flaunt it if you've got it" approach. It is more of simply knowing you are saved and letting yourself openly and unabashedly rejoice in the light of that truth.

Get comfortable with Christ

You and probably everyone you know have a comfortable pair of shoes. When wearing them, comfort is part of the experience. New shoes may become comfortable over time, but during the "breaking in" period they can be quite uncomfortable. We are not comparing Christ to an old shoe, but as Christians we need to be comfortable in our faith. Sharing the truth should be a comfortable fit to our position in Christ. And, like a new pair of shoes that become more comfortable with use, we become more comfortable with Christ as we walk with Him. We look forward to or remember those times when we come out of an uncomfortable pair of shoes and slip our feet into something more comfortable. We should be so comfortable in our relationship with Christ that talking with someone about Him and relating to them about what He has done in our life, is as natural as putting on our comfortable shoes. Those with whom you talk about Christ will observe your comfort level and be more at ease with you and any witnessing topic that comes up.

Remember "Whose you are"

A military attaché represents a department or some senior officer in the performance of duties assigned to the position. Everyone familiar with the program knows who is being represented, especially the attaché. No one doubts the authority involved and if there are any disputes, the attaché is not responsible for the outcome. As Christians, we must always be aware of who we represent. It is truly a "whose you are" type of thing. If we remember that we represent Christ, we can easily carry the message wherever and to whomever we are directed and let our "authority" assume the responsibility for the outcome. We must also understand that some of those with whom we share the truth will respond directly toward us and then knowing whose you are becomes even more important. There are those times when the message is not received well and the recipient will attempt to malign the attaché.

Operate in faith

When Christ returns we may all have an opportunity to follow Thomas and actually touch the body of our Lord and Savior and place our own hand into His side. But on this side of the Rapture (Christ's return for His Church), we must operate in faith, believing. Christ told Thomas, ". . . Stop doubting and believe." [29] We cannot expect to be heard or accepted if our own faith is weak. Our life as believers is a walk of faith. Regardless of where we are or the circumstance or situation confronting us, we are called by God to operate in faith.

Opportunities to Make Christ the Topic

Merriam-Webster identifies opportunity as a noun and defines it as: A favorable juncture of circumstances. Make a note of the word "favorable" in this definition. Christ is a most favorable part of any believer's life and making Him the topic when talking with others is the opportunity we want. So, when do these opportunities appear?

When someone asks

This is not an unusual occurrence. Living your life with Christ in front of others will generate questions. People will ask. You can depend on it. When it happens you need to be prepared with answers.

Remember what Peter wrote in his first general epistle, "Always be prepared to give an answer to everyone who asks you to give the reason for the hope that you have." [30]

When you're part of a conversation

In our fast moving society, finding yourself involved or participating in conversations about most anything, is not uncommon. Our lives are inter-tangled with the events of the moment and the impact of those events on our own lives. Conversation is a natural outlet and we are often caught up at lesser or greater levels in discussions about current events and regular day-to-day activities. Whether it is a one-on-one or multiple participant dialogue, conversations often turn toward spiritual and religious matters. At that moment, an opportunity has been presented.

Special problem(s)

Each day has a way of presenting its own set of problems. Often times this is passed off as life. Even so, in the process of living our daily lives, there are situations or circumstances that befall us or someone around us, that can only be described as a special problem. When the special problem belongs to another person, an opportunity to introduce the love and care of the Lord as a part of addressing the issue may be the direction you should take. Certainly not a time to adopt a "holier-than-thou" attitude. When it is your special problem it is also an opportunity to demonstrate your personal relationship with Christ. How you handle the problem is a testimony of your own faith walk with the Lord.

Employee/boss relationship(s)

In the work place there are relationships between employees and bosses. Gene Getz, in <u>The Measure of a Church</u>, wrote, "We may not be slaves, but many of us are employees! And if we have any witness at all, our employers know we are Christians. And they are watching our lives to see if what we profess makes a difference in our performance!" [c] The bosses are usually aware of their position and respond to employees in non-confrontational situations. Not always the case for certain, but in general this is the standard. Employees, on the other hand, are most usually subordinate to those in management or supervisory roles. Not as easy or convenient to talk "up the chain" of command. However, in many instances, bosses and employees enjoy personal as well as professional relationships. Working close with each other can produce occasions when following Christ's example is an appropriate tack.

> <u>Anecdote</u>: Bill and Tom are co-workers. They have equal status but different responsibilities within the company where they work. They are friends and have a good relationship with John, the owner of the company. Bill has come to Tom with a situation. He has an opportunity to obtain a critical component for one of the company's projects at an extremely low price. He suspects the transaction would actually be illegal, but the price would produce an attractive profit margin for the project and the company. He also suspects the source of the component is slightly clandestine.
>
> Tom is a Christian. He is aware of the competitive nature of their business and that John, the business owner, would be pleased if Bill's project was produced at a good price. Obviously Bill is looking forward to the positive response of the owner and the impact the project would have on his

career. Since Bill came to Tom with the situation, Tom has an opportunity to introduce his faith-based understanding of the situation.

Without responding in shock and amazement, Tom simply confirms his understanding of the opportunity as presented by Bill and relates the truth of the matter. "Bill, you will have to live with the outcome, good or bad. God has established guidelines for all of us to apply in our lives. We are not to be associated with anything that resembles fraud and we most certainly are not to knowingly be involved with anything that could bring harm or disrespect to others. John may be 'on board' with the process, but if the company comes to grief because of the acquisition of the component, you will be responsible. I encourage you to look elsewhere for the component and I know John will appreciate that course of action." Bill responded in a positive manner. He told Tom, "I know you are a Christian and I knew you would have an appropriate response. I agree and will find the component through a legitimate source."

Bill was successful in getting the necessary component at a good price and the project was completed. John became aware of the decision Bill made during the process of developing the product. He congratulated Bill on his "good" decision and rewarded him with more than a token bonus from the proceeds.

A question or comment can come from either the boss or the employee. Without compromise, the boss can respond to an employee's question. And, conversely, an employee or co-worker can respond to a question from either. Common sense goes a long way in determining when these types of conversations are acceptable. Taking the conversation away from the work place is also an appropriate course of action.

Current event(s)

Last night's news or today's paper can stab you with the recounting of a horrible situation or even elate you with the confirmation of something wonderful having occurred. With a complete and genuine understanding that neither category of events caught God by surprise, we can be prepared when current events lead us directly to an opportunity to make Christ the topic.

Calamity befalls us all. Whether it is personal or disassociated and involved with others, it happens. Talking about it can harden your heart and dampen your spirit, unless you accept God's position in the matter. He gave the prophet Nahum a vision and he wrote, "The Lord is good, a refuge in times of trouble. He cares for those who trust in Him." [31] We can apply this truth when addressing a negative experience in our own life or the lives of others. We can introduce, or reintroduce as the case may be, the truth written by the Apostle Matthew, that God ". . . causes His sun to rise on the evil and the good, and sends rain on the righteous and the unrighteous." [32]

Inner-family/relative relationships

Opportunities to share our faith are abundant within our own families. Probably not a major news flash that not all believers are blessed with having come from a Christ centered and faith nurturing family. With this fact in place, we know there are many believers who have close personal family members who have not accepted Christ. Even though the Gospel message of salvation may be difficult to present to these loved ones, as believers, we have a serious desire to let our families know the truth. Who is better to tell them than one who is part of the family?

How do you do it?

I have never physically seen Jesus but I have seen Him in my life and in the lives of others.

Like the Apostle Paul, "I do not understand what I do. For what I want to do I do not do, but what I hate I do." [33] I wrestle with these questions and like most everyone; I do and think the things I should not, and don't do the things I should. God is faithful to His promise and when I go to Him, confess my shortcomings, He forgives and I am rejuvenated in my spirit and begin anew. This is a continual process for all believers. Not one of us is perfect. Only Christ is perfect. We are to follow His example. As He told Peter, He is telling us, "Feed my sheep." [34] So, in the process of making Christ the topic, how do you do it? The following are suggestions that address this question.

Ask questions you can answer

Example

> Question: If today becomes your last day alive on the earth and you stand before God who asks why He should allow you into His Kingdom, what would you say? [d]

> Answer: Anything less than claiming salvation through the sacrifice of Christ, is at best an incorrect answer.

You are not getting ready for a debate. You are preparing to present the Gospel of Jesus Christ unabashedly and with conviction. Do not place yourself into a situation where you go into an encounter with a lost person unawares. If the person to whom you are witnessing asks a question that you cannot immediately answer, recognize it and request an opportunity to think it over and get back later with your answer. But, when you pose a question, be sure you have a defendable answer. When you know the answer it is easy to identify a wrong response.

Be positive

Ever been approached by someone trying to sell something with an opening comment of "You wouldn't want to buy a *whatever*, would you?" Very quickly, your answer is No. We aren't "selling" anything, but if we approach people in a negative manner, even if we are representing the Savior of the world, we will most assuredly receive a negative response. In math, multiplying two negatives produces a positive. If you equate positive with coming on strong, you can most always depend on it coming across negative. Positive means "not negative." You may be positive that what you are saying is true, but if you push it on someone, it will not be accepted positively. Think Christ-like. Who could be more positive?

Be honest

It is much easier to say you don't know than to pretend you do and then have to defend an undefendable position. The end to a conversation based on a falsehood is your embarrassment with ridicule being focused on Christ. Stay focused on the truth, both in the teller and in the telling. Scripture is true. Even the difficult passages are true, and God did not allow the writers to embellish them, omit them, or gloss them over.

Use your own experience(s)

Before you were saved you were lost. Doesn't make any difference whether your salvation experience came early or late. Before you weren't and now you are. J. Vernon McGee put it this way, "There are only two types of people on topside of the earth: Saints and Aint's." [e] Use what God has given you and tell others about it.

Your life and the experiences from it are uniquely yours. You will be more believable and convincing when talking with someone about the Lord if your comments are based on truth from personal recollections and/or experiences. This does not exclude references to Scripture or comments by others. It just means your life speaks for you. Especially if you are talking with someone who has observed you for some period of time. (That person may have known you before you were born again).

Agree, but don't compromise

We have all heard the old statement about "agreeing to disagree." It is a real position we may have to accept at times. When you are witnessing to someone or sharing the truth of the Gospel, it may become necessary that you simply agree that you are not in agreement. This will also eliminate any air of compromise and possibly provide an opportunity to talk again at a future date.

> Anecdote: Remember Bill and Tom? They are the co-workers who discussed an integrity question at their work place. Their relationship involves more than that

one incident. Tom is a mature Christian, grounded in the Word, and he has been living his life in front of Bill for a few years. Bill is a "borderline Christian." He has accepted Christ but his growth in the Lord has been hampered by his "it has to make sense to me" attitude.

Tom has been discussing Biblical perspectives with Bill. One concept that creates an intense level of discussion is the absolute authority of God's Word. An example Bill uses is that God's Word says Lot's wife was turned into a pillar of salt. He cannot accept that and argues that whoever wrote it was only embellishing the story for effect.

Tom has regularly shared with Bill the importance of the authority of God's Word. He refers Bill to the words of Peter, who wrote in his second general epistle, "Above all, you must understand that no prophecy of Scripture came about by the prophet's own interpretation. For prophecy never had its origin in the will of man, but men spoke from God as they were carried along by the Holy Spirit." [33] God's Word is specific about what happened to Lot's wife. Moses, as the author/compiler of the Pentateuch, wrote in Genesis, "But Lot's wife looked back, and she became a pillar of salt." [34] Bill cannot get his mind around the concept and puts it into the category of 'things of faith' he cannot accept. His argument is one of simple common sense and that the passage is only an allegory.

Tom, without compromise, simply reminds Bill that this is an area where they will have to agree to disagree. It doesn't inhibit Tom with his on-going dialogue with Bill and Bill is not threatened. Truth is always in the mix and available for Bill to accept as he grows in faith.

Address the topic at hand

"Wanderitis" should be avoided, especially in outreach and witnessing. Staying on target and on topic is very important. When you are attempting to affirm or confirm a faith or fact-based position, you will lose emphasis and most likely your trend of thought if you wander off-point. You also run the risk of confusing the issue at hand. Make a mental note of the side-tracking element and come back to it later, if needed.

> <u>Anecdote</u>: Let's look in on Tom and Bill again. Both are sports enthusiasts and enjoy any opportunity to discuss sports related topics. Bill brings up the subject of a well-known professional athlete who became involved in gambling and other unsavory activities. The athlete has been barred from any further contact with the sport, which deprives the sport and the fans of having this athlete's involvement. Bill says no one was hurt and thinks the athlete should be forgiven and repatriated with his organization and receive any and all awards that have been stripped away or denied. He asks Tom what he thinks about the situation.
>
> Tom knows this is an opportunity to shore-up some Christian principles with Bill and waits for the right time to come into the conversation. Tom suggests the situation with the athlete is much like the "original sin" situation with Adam and Eve. God established the rules. They chose to ignore them. Should the athlete be forgiven? Certainly. Rewarded? Absolutely not. Bill comes back with "How long must the athlete be punished? He was an excellent athlete and his accomplishments should not go unheralded. What about . . . ," and Bill begins mentioning other "outstanding athletes" who have gone a bit off

course who are still in the game. Tom is also aware of and mentions several folks who have gone "off the reservation" and who are still viable in their respective fields.

Bill and Tom are now off-topic. They have wandered away from the principle position Tom was beginning to share and have focused their discussion toward issues that are irrelevant to Bill's original question. The momentum of the moment has been lost and it will be difficult to turn the discussion back to the real issue of obeying the rules and accepting the consequences when we do not.

Get on common ground

You do not need to adopt the habits or life-styles of anyone or any specific group to be an effective witness. But finding an area of common ground will help. Someone with whom you wish to share the truth of Christ may be a social out-cast, or worse, but if you observe that person for a while, you may discover an area in their life that could be considered "common ground." Using that particular element could open the door of opportunity for you to come along side, claim the common ground and introduce that person to Jesus Christ. It is similar in many ways to building a bridge. You are on one side of a question and the person with whom you want to witness is on the other. Once the bridge is in place, you can get to common ground. If you leave the bridge in place, it becomes easier for the one to whom you are witnessing to cross over. Sounds simple enough, but it takes commitment, work and a proper attitude.

Whatever works for you

When it is all said and done, how you do it comes down to whatever works for you. All the encouragement and instruction in the world won't help if you are not a participant. Give yourself the benefit of some time to think about what you want to do. Do the work and become comfortable with yourself and then be about it. Be the person God wants you to be. Keep your eye on the target and remember "Whose" you are.

Questions

When you are involved in outreach or just witnessing to a friend, but particularly when you are moving toward your objective of making Christ the topic, you will come upon multiple opportunities to address straight-up as well as off-the-wall questions. Some of them will be silly and some will test your faith. The following are examples. Not the rule, just examples.

Have you ever actually seen Jesus?

No. But I see evidence of Him everywhere. I have never seen Abraham Lincoln, but no one would argue his having been here. History confirms his reality. History also confirms Jesus and records the evidence of His resurrection. He told the Apostle Thomas, "Because you have seen me, you have believed; blessed are those who have not seen and yet have believed." [37] Even if the writings of Scripture had not been compiled into the Bible, the historical writings would still be available to us. You must deny history to deny the existence of Jesus Christ.

Where was Jesus when God was creating things?

Jesus has always been. He, along with the Holy Spirit, is part of the GODHEAD. "Let us make human beings in our image, in our likeness . . . ,"[38] are words from God given to Moses to be written in the Book of Beginnings. Who is the "our image" in this statement? Pretty clear from this that God the Father, God the Son (Jesus) and God the Holy Spirit, have always been God. And from this we can see that Jesus was very much involved in the Creation process.

So, God is the Father, the Holy Spirit is the Mother, and Jesus is the Son?

No. God is uniquely God in three distinct personalities. It seems to be the aim of many to force God into the image of man rather than accepting God at His Word as the Creator. The True God of the Bible is **God as the Father**, creating all there is **as God the Son** and ministering to His creation **as God the Holy Spirit**.

Not that God can be described so simply, but think of a three-legged milking stool. Exactly fit for its purpose and operating with three legs. Won't work with two, or even one leg missing. A true triune-entity. One God: Father, Son and Holy Spirit. In his final greeting and benediction to the Believers in Corinth, the Apostle Paul wrote, "May the grace of the Lord Jesus Christ, and the love of God, and the fellowship of the Holy Spirit be with you all." [39] These words leave no doubt as to the identity of God.

Why is God so hard to find?

He isn't. God has made His presence known throughout the history of man. He is available anywhere at any time. It is man who has determined that God is hard to find. In an attempt to find God on his terms, man has established himself as the authority for determining who God is. When God's plan does not fit into man's plan, he has created a new god, or multiple gods to accommodate the ilks and ways of man. The Apostle John, in his Revelation, included the words of the Lord telling the Laodiceans, and others who might read it, "Here I am! I stand at the door and knock. If anyone hears My voice and opens the door, I will come in . . ." [40] Doesn't sound like God is too difficult to find. He is at the door to your heart and mind.

Isn't God in everything?

God is omnipresent, but as Tim Temple suggests in *Pantheism's Concept of God's Omnipresence*, "most people are uncomfortable with the omnipresence of God, and so because of that, down through the years men have developed various concepts of His presence. People know that God is present with us, but we try to work our way around it. One concept of omnipresence is *pantheism*. Pantheism says that God is *in* everything, that everything is in God. That sounds like omnipresence, doesn't it? That does say that God is present, but there is a very subtle change in there in pantheism, and that is to say that God is *in* everything; everything is *in* God. What that does is reduce God to an impersonal force. He is everywhere present, but He is a personal kind of presence." [f] Nothing is more personal than your relationship with Christ.

Aren't there many ways to find God? After all, the majority of the world's population is non-Christian.

Regardless of how old one believes the world is, everyone can accept the fact that it has been around a long time. Even with the cataclysmic event of an all-encompassing flood, man has been around a long time as well. Cultures developed along with similar, yet different, understandings as to how or why "all this happened." Religion, rightly or wrongly, took up the cause of determining who and what God is. And, these cultures constructed complex systems to support their beliefs. Today there are thousands of these "systems" around the world.

God, who created the first man and loved him and his descendants enough to protect them through the devastation of a worldwide flood, also loves us enough today to provide a way for us to access Him. History records an era when those who took God at His Word, believed the truth and accepted Christ by faith, were called Christians. In, or near 60 AD, the Apostle Paul recorded this fact when he wrote, "The disciples were called Christians first at Antioch." [41] There are many today who traffic in this name. Some though, have distorted the truth to fit their own particular program lending to confusion. But the Truth is still true: Christ is the only way to have a personal and eternal relationship with God.

Isn't Allah just another name for the same God?

No, Allah is not just another name for God. As instructed by God in the first of the original Ten Commandments, ". . . You shall have no other gods before Me." [42] It is not a suggestion.

The earthly history of man traces everyone to Adam; the first man and the first human created by God. From Adam we can trace mankind's history to the present. Along the way we find Abraham the father of Ishmael and Isaac. These were half-brothers from different mothers. God told Abraham, "My covenant I will establish with Isaac." [43] God did not forget Ishmael, He also told Abraham, "As for Ishmael, I have heard you; behold, I will bless him, and will make him fruitful and will multiply him exceedingly . . ." [44]

Muhammad, (Circa 700 AD), a descendant of Ishmael, has brought more than one billion people to his side of a 4,000 year old conflict through the religion of Islam. Arab Christians and pagans used the word *Ilah* for God. If and when used by Arabic speaking individuals it can be considered to be a name for the same God (YHWH[*]) who is speaking to mankind in His Word. The word "Allah" is likely a contraction of the Arabic *Al-ilah*, which doesn't necessarily mean "The God." So, no, Allah is not just another name for God.

---

[*] This is four Hebrew letters (Yod, He, Waw and He) called the "Tetragrammaton". The four characters are the four Hebrew letters that correspond to YHWH and are transliterated *IAUE* or *Yahweh*. Yahweh is the name of the Almighty Father in Heaven that people commonly call "The LORD" or "God". Muhammad would have known this, but in the Qur'an he used the Arabic word *Allah*.

CHAPTER SEVEN

WRAP IT UP. GIVE IT AWAY

When God saved you, He gave you a gift with the understanding that it was something you could never lose, but at the same time it is something He wants you to share at every appropriate opportunity. We know from God's Word that our salvation is not of our doing and that it is something we have to accept. Christ put the finishing touches on the work that had to be done on our behalf, and by His effort alone we have the gift of eternal life. And, as unseemly as it might sound, there are those who actually refuse to accept His gift. Christ said, ". . . I have come that they(you) may have life, and have it to the full."[1] The gift of eternal life with God is available for the asking.

Those of us who have this truth in our lives have the ability to share it with others. One way to do this is to "package" our own understanding of this priceless gift so that others may see what we have and ask us to let them know what they might do to have a similar experience in their lives. When they do, having a personal testimony of God's work in our life is a good way to package the message so we can give it away, repeatedly.

Our role in this effort is defining the package and putting it together. To do that requires some attention to detail and a willingness to be honest with ourselves while we prepare to be honest with others. If we work through this, we can have a very rewarding experience in the process. Let's take a look at some of the questions that need to be asked and answered, as well as some the steps associated with our "package."

What's in a Package?

Before anyone can wrap it up, it is pretty important to know what you are wrapping. For the purpose of this effort, we need to understand there is no cut and dried formula for what goes into a testimony.

We simply need to organize our thoughts around the process and develop a way to share what God has done in our life. In Peter's first general epistle he wrote, "But in your hearts set apart Christ as Lord. Always be prepared to give an answer to everyone who asks you to give the reason for the hope that you have. But do this with gentleness and respect." [2] Generally, a testimony will have a few simple components comprised of: An opening statement; some simple background information; a reflection on what God did; and a report of what happened.

An **opening statement** should be direct and could include a few points relative to your personal situation. Without any fanfare or artificial excitement, in your own words you can express how:

- **God heard you** and answered your prayer.
  ". . . The Lord is near to all who call on Him, . . . He hears their cry and saves them." [3]

- **Christ responded** as promised and came into your life.
  "Let us hold unswervingly to the hope we profess, for He who promised is faithful." [4]

  ". . . if anyone hears my voice and opens the door, I will come in . . ." [5]

- **God knew** just where to find you.
  "Can anyone hide in secret places so that I cannot see him?" [6]

- **Your life was** (describe how your life was before), then,
  ". . . when we were controlled by the sinful nature, the sinful passions aroused by the law were at work in our bodies, so that we bore fruit for death." [7]

- **As a witness**, simply ask, "May I share something with you?" *"Therefore, if anyone is in Christ, he is a new creation; the old has gone, the new has come!"* [8]

Some **simple background information** is now required. You need to relate:

- **When you were saved.** It's a bench mark for you and for them. The most important event in your life is certainly memorable. You get the joy of remembering, they get to hear that you know the exact moment. (If you cannot fix a date, fix a circa. Reaffirm your own position with Christ and go forward). How absolutely wonderful it is to tell someone else what the Lord Jesus Christ has done for you. Then you can truthfully say to anyone with whom you are sharing, "He will do the same for you."
- **Where you were saved.** No need for embellishment. Wherever it was it was a real place and God was there with you.
- **Circumstance** at the moment you were saved. Influence of others on your life at the time. Work place, social arena, whatever.
- **Situation** of the moment when you were saved. Your attitude toward the circumstances around you. Physical, emotional, psychological.

Now you can reflect on **what God did**.

- **God drew you to Himself.** Drawn by God the Father, you became aware of Him. "You did not choose Me, but I chose you . . ." [9]

- **Convicted by the Holy Spirit.** Your mind and heart changed. You became open to the idea of eternity and where you might spend it.

- *Saved by the Lord Jesus Christ*. As promised. You applied:
  - *Faith*—the vehicle of salvation

    "*. . . faith is being sure of what we hope for and certain of what we do not see.*" [10]

  - *Response to the invitation*—asked Christ to come in

    "*Everyone who calls on the name of the Lord will be saved.*" [11]

  - *Belief*—took action

    "*. . . whoever hears My word and believes Him who sent Me has eternal life and will not be condemned; he has crossed over from death to life.*" [12]

Then tell them **what happened**.

- *Your life was changed*. The life you had before depended on you and what you thought. Now your life depends on Christ and what He thinks.

  "*I have been crucified with Christ and I no longer live, but Christ lives in me. The life I live in the body, I live by faith in the Son of God, who loved me and gave Himself for me.*" [13]

- *Jesus Christ is now a reality in your life*. "What would Jesus do" is more than an engraving on a wrist bracelet, or some other piece of jewelry. It is an applicable question to most any part of your life.

  "*My sheep listen to my voice; I know them, and they follow Me.*" [14]

How Do You Wrap It?

Getting your thoughts into a package is very similar to wrapping a physical package. Think about it. You want your package to be:

- *Attractive*—Not gaudy or so flashy it compromises what's inside. If your wrapping gets all the attention, you have wasted your time. What you have to share is special. Use common, every-day words. You want the contents to be well received. If you go in with "You won't believe what happened to me," they probably won't. But, "I really had something unique happen in my life," can set the stage for the next category.
- *Different*—Not odd, just different. If your package appears to be the same as all the others, you will receive a "ho hum" response. "Oh, that's what they all say." You want your package to be enough different that it will be considered as:
- *Individual*—Your style. Not an attempt to copy another person's technique or mannerisms. Be yourself. You are uniquely you and God accepted you just as you are.

And be:

- *Specific*—To the point. No rabbit trails. Don't be glib or mess around with non-essential information. If you coat your message with a lot of whimsical stuff, you will not be taken seriously.

Why Wrap It Anyway?

A gift as important as the salvation message should be presented appropriately when and where it is needed. We want to wrap it for several reasons, but most importantly because this particular present is:

- *A special gift*—Bought and paid for with the blood of Jesus Christ the Lord. No other gift like it anywhere at any price. Completely unique. And it's yours to share.

"For God so loved the world that He gave His one and only Son, that whoever believes in Him shall not perish but have eternal life." [15]

- **It is worthy**—The sacrifice of the Giver makes this gift worthy beyond whatever manner or method we could use for the wrapping, but it should be wrapped to honor the giving. *"Greater love has no one than this, that he lay down his life for his friends."* [16]

- **It should be protected**—Flippancy of thought or action detracts from the gift. Wrapping it for giving protects the message until it is ready to be opened and shared. *"Let no one deceive you with empty words, . . ."* [17]

- **It is exciting to open**—How excited were you to learn that the gift of eternal life is yours? When the present is wrapped, then you can look forward to sharing that excitement with others when they allow you to present the gift you have for them. *"Everyone was filled with awe, . . ."* [18]

What Makes It Mine?

A significant part of preparing the present is making it yours. It becomes your personal gift when you draw from areas of your own life and include them in the process. A general reading of the Pauline letters [19] will expose you to many of the experiences the Apostle Paul shared with others during his missionary journeys. Your experiences, words and enthusiasm are three specific areas of your life which may contribute the information you need to prepare and personalize your package.

Anecdote: Due to a family situation, it became necessary for a believer to relocate himself and his family to another city. This was going to be a major career adjustment and after bathing the entire situation in prayer a request for transfer was submitted. Since it was a professional matter, the entire program and process had to be accepted and approved by principals in both operational locations and by all affected personnel. One-by-one the principals agreed and approved the transfer. Not only did they approve it, they offered to cover the cost as well. Totally unexpected.

With approvals in place all that was needed then was for the details to be worked out. There were lots of details, but selling an existing home during a "down market" period and finding suitable housing in the new city, were the most impacting. The believer had surrendered the situation to God at the onset. So, one might guess the outcome.

With God's obvious involvement, the existing home was under contract in three weeks, at the asking price and with a 90-day closing window. Ample amount of time to locate a house in the new city. With 60-days gone and thirty to go, nothing had been found. Cause for alarm? Maybe. But, not when God is your primary real estate agent. Specific to the search was the need for the replacement property to provide at a minimum, the space required, a fenced yard and be available within the requisite price range, and if possible on a cul-de-sac.

A family member located in the new city, out on an unscheduled walk noticed a property advertisement, jotted down the number and made it available. During the call it was discovered that the property would be available at the end of the current month (within the 30-day window); physically the property was a three-bedroom, two-bath, two-car garage with a fenced back yard; available on a lease-purchase option in the price range required; and located on a cul-de-sac.

God was also involved in all the other areas associated with the relocation. The movers came, packed, loaded and delivered the contents to the new house, all within the time-frame allowed for the effort.

Easy for unbelievers and doubters to say the situation would have worked itself out anyway. Not likely, but some will say God had nothing to do with it. Perhaps. But the family member who took the unscheduled walk had never walked that particular route before. The current occupant of the new house had just become involved in a situation that required an immediate move. And, nothing had been available during the previous 60-days. Coincidence? Now add to the equation that the new house was close to the local family member, which was a primary reason for the relocation, and the house was close to church, close to the work place, and close to community services. Difficult to claim coincidence with all those elements in play. And, don't forget, it had a fenced yard and was on a cul-de-sac.

We all have experiences. Regardless of your age, as a believer, you have pre and post-salvation experiences. It may take a few moments of self-reflection to capture some of those experiences in a manner compatible with the objective. You can pare out some of the better or more interesting experiences and include them in your present. Be specific in your effort and select from your experiences incidences that demonstrate the key role God has played in your life. A mirror may provide some assistance in this effort. When you gaze into it, you will notice someone looking back that bears a remarkable resemblance to you. A mirror presents a reflection of you and provides an opportunity for some self analysis. You can ask the person looking back at you some very serious questions without fear of the answers. Not necessarily warm and fuzzy answers, but without any fear.

Words play a large part in your "gifting process." The more the words are your own the better. You will be more comfortable in the telling of any experiences you have if they are recounted in your own words. Those with whom you share your gift will appreciate it more when you use your own words to express the details associated with your walk with the Lord.

Enthusiasm is also an important part of your package. When you call on your experiences and use your own words in making an account, you should be enthusiastic in your presentation. Dull doesn't do as well as excitement. And those who hear will be more receptive if you come to them with a positive attitude bathed in enthusiasm.

Tie a Bow on It!

With your present put together, it's time to put on the ribbon and tie a bow on it. This part of the gift says something about you right up front. It also says something about the contents before it gets opened. It doesn't have to be flashy or pretentious, but it needs to draw attention to your gift. And, with a pretty good bow in place, you can easily identify your own present. The Apostle Paul's missionary letter from Rome to the believers at Philippi encouraged them to "Let your gentleness be evident to all, ..."[20] The following are suggestions that could be used as "bows" to help put your gift to work. Read them aloud; alone or to another person. You need to hear, more than just see the words.

- Hi. Never know who you're going to meet at (Activity / Event). I'm a Christian. I try to be a witness wherever I go. Please read this. (Present Tract or whatever). If you have questions I may be able to provide some answers.
- (Person's Name), you've been my friend a long time. I've wanted to share something with you for a while now. I'm a Christian and I want you to know what my personal relationship with Jesus Christ is all about.
- (Person's Name), we've been working together for some time. There's something special in my life I've wanted to share with you. I'm a Christian and I want you to know what my personal relationship with Jesus Christ is all about.
- (Person's Name), you've been/you're going through some difficult situations. I'm not sure I understand, but I want you to know I care. I'm a Christian and I know Jesus wants you to have peace in your mind and heart. May I share some of this truth with you?
- (Person's Name), now that I know you a little better, I feel comfortable sharing a part of my life that really makes me aware of who I am. I'm a Christian and because of my personal relationship with Jesus Christ, I have a real purpose in being here. I'd like to share with you just how special Christ is. Could I do that right now?
- (Person's Name), I see from your (outfit/mannerisms) that you're a (name of whatever). I'm a Christian. I try to be a witness wherever I go. Has anyone ever taken an opportunity to discuss with you what it means to be a Christian? Could I do that now?
- (Person's Name), I know you agree the Bible is a very special book, but has anyone ever shown you what it says about eternal security? It's a fascinating topic and God has a lot to say about it. It will only take a few minutes to look at a couple passages. We can talk more about it later.

- (Person's Name), can you imagine what it would be like in this world without God? His Book? His Son? I'm a Christian and sharing Christ with others is my most favorite thing to do. Have you ever heard about these things?

Who Gets It?

With your gift wrapped and ready to be shared, you may want to work through the process a few times before you step into the world's arena. There are several opportunities available for you to open your present and share it. Some are much less threatening than just going "cold" into a witnessing experience.

The least threatening would be with others at your local church, as part of an outreach group. In this forum you could rehearse your presentation and role play with other believers. This builds confidence and experience and enables all participants to become comfortable with the "telling." This should not be considered a drama or acting group. This is a time when you can be with like-minded brothers and sisters and cultivate an attitude of openness while you become encouraged in and with your ability to share your faith.

The next step, or perhaps even a first step, would be to establish a "witness tree." This can be as easy as making a list or a simple diagram that identifies family members, friends, neighbors, work associates, and others. This is definitely not a list of targets. It is a tool to assist your thinking about who is in your "tree." You can mention these individuals in your prayer time as you prepare to be involved in the work. Remember the importance of prayer? As it was with the Apostle Paul when he wrote to the Thessalonians and encouraged them to "pray continually," [21] when you have individuals in your prayer thoughts, they are part of your life. Then, when God puts the opportunity in your path you will be there for them.

Anecdote: An older man, let's call him Jim, was mild mannered and completely non-confrontational in his attitude toward others. Especially around those with whom he worked. He had survived some serious health issues, not the least of which was heart by-pass surgery, and as a result he was somewhat frail in his appearance. As a believer Jim was also convinced he had a responsibility to tell others about the saving grace of the Lord Jesus Christ. Jim worked in a multi-story office building and as part of his physical therapy he took to the stairwell each day during his lunch break. He would ride the elevator to the tenth floor where he would access the stairwell and walk down. During his trips down the stairwell he would encounter folks on their way up in the stairwell and greet them with a soft, three-word testimony:

"God saved me."

Most would ignore his statement. Some would smile in obvious agreement or amazement. Others though, would respond with "What did you say?" "What was that?" or, "What do you mean by that?" With that, or whatever returning comment came his way, Jim was able to share his faith and introduce many folks to Christ.

It is just that easy to share Christ with another person. No need for pomp or ceremony. Just an available and spontaneous spirit directed toward a lost and dying world. Your name doesn't have to be Jim and you don't need to suffer through open heart surgery to be encouraged by the fact that God has something for you to do in the furtherance of His truth in the world today.

Points to Consider

As you move forward with your commitment to be involved in an outreach ministry, whether individually, or as part of a group, there are some points in the process you may wish to consider:

- You appreciate another person's position or comment if it is relevant to where you are or have been.

  The Apostle Paul had been on many journeys. His experiences were numerous and he knew much about the suffering and disappointment of those to whom he spoke. Even in Jerusalem, after he had been seized in the Temple, he was able to share his position with the Jews and the Romans. Dr. Luke provides an account of such preaching by Paul, in his documentary writings in the Book of Acts. "Then Paul said: 'I am a Jew, born in Tarsus of Cilicia, but brought up in this city . . . . I was thoroughly trained in the law of our fathers and was just as zealous for God as any of you are today. I persecuted the followers of this Way to their death, arresting both men and women and throwing them into prison, as also the high priest and all the Council can testify. I even obtained letters from them to their brothers in Damascus, and went there to bring these people as prisoners to Jerusalem to be punished.'" [22]

- Attractive and pleasant or unusual presents (testimonies) are non-threatening. They are also more easily delivered.
- The bow used to tie up a package (testimony) says something about the person who wrapped it, more than what is in the gift box.
- Your testimony needs to be "your testimony." Not a make over of someone else's.

- No matter how you became a Believer, you have a testimony.
- If you have always been a Christian, then your own experiences are a testimony.
- You earn the privilege of sharing your faith by listening—not by arguing.
- If someone just wants to argue, defer your testimony.

Don't invest your time with meaningless banter. In his second letter to Timothy, the Apostle Paul wrote, "Avoid godless chatter, because those who indulge in it will become more and more ungodly." [23]

- If you do become involved in and argument, then agree to only argue or discuss one point at a time.

Example of God's Special Touch

When you are contemplating your personal testimony, give yourself the benefit of setting aside some time to think about it. As you mull over the telling of the events associated with our own personal salvation experience, remember these thought steps: 1) Christ is the theme, always, 2) Look to Christ for everything, and 3) Put your present together in faith.

An outline could be helpful with this effort. Here is an example:

1. Opening statement
   1. Uncomplicated
   2. Flows out of you
2. Simple background data
   1. When and where
   2. Circumstance and situation

    3. What God did
       1. Conviction
       2. Salvation
    4. Then what?
       1. Growth
       2. Christ in me and through me

Following this outline your simple testimony can just flow out of you and onto paper.

1. Opening Statement

    1. *Uncomplicated* ~ It's still amazing to me, how God uses real life situations to direct the lives of those He has created. Sometimes we aren't aware He is doing it. My experience in this is still fresh on my mind, even though the "particular situation" occurred some time ago.
    2. *Flows out of you* ~ It's not that my situation was so unique, or anything. It's just the way things happened to make me realize how much God really loved me. It's also a testimony of how stubborn a person can be in dealing with the spiritual portion of his life.

2. Simple Background Data

    1. *When and where* ~ In October 1971, I was hospitalized as a result of a severe reaction to penicillin.
    2. *Circumstance and situation* ~ I was paralyzed and thoroughly confused about the whole thing. Medicine prescribed by my doctor caused a problem and I refused to take any additional doses. That didn't set well with the doctor or the hospital staff. When confronted with the situation, they told me if I didn't take the medication I could die. With those kind

words, they left and I was alone. Alone with my thoughts and a fairly good understanding of the circumstances.

3. *What God did* ~ Well into the night, I lay there contemplating my fate. I was not prepared for the possibilities. My life sort of passed in review. What did all this mean? Why me God? I hadn't really thought much about Him until then. I wasn't trying to blame anyone. I just wanted to know why. (The truth of Christ had been presented to me previously). The more I tried to get hold of the situation the more confused I became. Then something happened. My entire attention was drawn to the truth. God was right there with me.

   1. *Conviction* ~ I became aware in my spirit, down deep where I live, that there is truly a God and that His Son, Jesus Christ, had died for my mistakes.
   2. *Salvation* ~ I told God I accepted Him on His terms and that I wanted another chance to live. I asked Jesus to save me and live His life through me. And I cried. In fact I cried myself to sleep.

4. *Then what* ~ When I awoke the next morning, the Holy Spirit brought to mind what had taken place during the night. I confirmed it in my spirit and a peace beyond understanding came over me. I was sure, that no matter what, I belonged to Christ.

   1. *Growth* ~ Since that life changing experience, Christ has used many new and challenging situations to help me grow in faith.
   2. *Christ in me and through me* ~ His hand has guided me along major paths and sustained my whole family during some tough and not so tough times. Without Jesus, I can honestly say my life wouldn't be.

Note: This is only an example of a testimony. Your testimony is your own. Use your life and the life God has called you to for the words you need to tell others about Christ's life. The truth is more exciting than any story you could ever make up. It is real for you, so simply share the reality of your faith by putting what God has done for you into your own words. Those you tell will be more easily convinced because of the sincerity in your story. When you are living out your testimony in front of them, those who see it will know it for what it is, *TRUTH*. As the Apostle John wrote in his gospel, ". . . you will know the truth, and the truth will set you free." [24]

Now you can re-write your testimony without the outline form and have it ready if/when you need it. (Read it over multiple times, until you become so familiar with it you can call it up, in whole or in parts, in your mind, whenever needed).

> It's still amazing to me, how God uses real life situations to direct the lives of those He has created. Sometimes we aren't aware He is doing it. My experience in this is still fresh on my mind, even though the "particular situation" occurred some time ago.

> It's not that my situation was so unique, or anything. It's just the way things happened to make me realize how much God really loved me. It's also a testimony of how stubborn a person can be in dealing with the spiritual portion of his life.

> In October 1971, I was hospitalized as a result of a severe reaction to penicillin.

> I was paralyzed and thoroughly confused about the whole thing. Medicine prescribed by my doctor caused a problem and I refused to take any additional doses. That

didn't set well with the doctor or the hospital staff. When confronted with the situation, they told me if I didn't take the medication I could die. With those kind words, they left and I was alone. Alone with my thoughts and a fairly good understanding of the circumstances.

Well into the night, I lay there contemplating my fate. I was not prepared for the possibilities. My life sort of passed in review. What did all this mean? Why me God? I hadn't really thought much about Him until then. I wasn't trying to blame anyone, I just wanted to know why. (The truth of Christ had been presented to me previously). The more I tried to get hold of the situation the more confused I became. Then something happened. My entire attention was drawn to the truth. God was right there with me.

I became aware in my spirit, down deep where I live, that there is truly a God and that His Son, Jesus Christ, had died for my mistakes.

I told God I accepted Him on His terms and that I wanted another chance to live. I asked Jesus to save me and live His life through me. And I cried. In fact I cried myself to sleep.

When I awoke the next morning, the Holy Spirit brought to mind what had taken place during the night. I confirmed it in my spirit and a peace beyond understanding came over me. I was sure, that no matter what, I belonged to Christ.

Since that life changing experience, Christ has used many new and challenging situations to help me grow in faith.

His hand has guided me along major paths and sustained my whole family during some tough and not so tough times. Without Jesus, I can honestly say my life wouldn't be.

Through the years that have passed since my own salvation experience, many opportunities have become available for growing in faith and sharing the Living Truth of Christ. All were not seized or recognized, but those that were are major milestones in this believer's life.

There have been times when attempting to witness to a fellow worker resulted in heated arguments about who God is and why He would allow a little child to be abused by a deranged person, or worse. Agnostics and atheists have attempted to befuddle the Gospel presentation with out-of-sync questions and nonsensical clamorings and innuendos. Real questions that demand real answers are part of the witnessing experience. We do not and cannot hope to know all the answers. But, we can commit ourselves to faithfully following the path that God has chosen for us by first accepting Him then allowing His will to be part of our coming in and going out.

By taking a few minutes to reduce your testimony to writing, you will have the opportunity of thought about the most significant event in your life. This is not a simple homework assignment. This is a life assignment for your personal response to what God has called you to do. Writing down your thoughts so you can organize them into a simple testimony of what you know God has done will give you the freedom to tell anyone, anytime, anywhere, about your personal relationship with the Savior. DO IT!

Questions

Make time regularly to ask yourself questions about your faith walk with the Lord. You can be certain Ol' what's his name has his agents working overtime to plant seeds of confusion and distortion into the minds and souls of those who will be placed in your path. Remember the encouragement Peter shared in his first general epistle. "Be self-controlled and alert. Your enemy the Devil prowls around like a roaring lion looking for someone to devour. Resist him, standing firm in the faith, because you know that your brothers (*and sisters*) throughout the world are undergoing the same kind of sufferings." [25] *GWTLW.*

God's Word The Last Word

CHAPTER EIGHT

PERSONAL TESIMONY

God's Personal Touch On

Wylie Comp

Called as an evangelist in 1978, Wylie has carried the message of Christ across the United States and into the United Kingdom. As Director of Faith Harvest Ministries, Inc. in Springfield, MO, he presents a seven-session, discussion-based seminar on outreach and witnessing to churches and Christian groups.

TESTIMONY

Wylie Comp

Sometimes it's difficult to know where you're going unless you can appreciate where you have been. As a Christian, I believe it would be more accurate to say, "You can't know where you have been unless you appreciate where you know you are going."

My appreciation originates with my parents. A Godly mother and an extremely principled father provided more than instruction, they presented an example. An example I would be drawn to during my growing-up years and call on as I stepped into the responsibilities of manhood. In that process I passed through multiple life-station events that confirm God's involvement in and around my life prior to my accepting and requesting Christ to come into it. One particular life-station event was aboard a U. S. Navy aircraft carrier during the era of the Viet Nam War. A small amount of history with a bit of fact data makes an appropriate backdrop.

My father was a member of the "Greatest Generation," and his love of country wasn't wasted on either of his sons. But I had a strong aversion to spending, or possibly donating my life for an ill-defined military objective on foreign soil. Several of my schoolmates had returned from the conflict in a "body bag." I had lost my deferment and held a low Selective Service Lottery Number, so being drafted became a serious concern.

Fortunately, or not, I secured one of only two positions available in the U. S. Naval Reserves at the Naval Air Station near my home, with a good understanding I would be satisfying my military obligation as an Air-Dale Reservist in the Navy. So much for those good thoughts.

Immediately after my return from Boot Camp and Specialty Training as an Aviation Ordinanceman, the North Koreans, in conjunction with the Russians and the Red Chinese, attacked and commandeered the *U.S.S. Pueblo*. Our government necessarily felt compelled to make a demonstrative response which included my Naval Air Reserve Squadron being called to active duty and being deployed on the U.S.S. Ranger, CVA-61, a Forrestal Class Aircraft Carrier.

War is Hell and even though our squadron was afloat and not "in country" with our troops on the ground, we were active and aggressively involved in the program. During Carrier Qualifications our operations were conducted 24/7. Launching and recovery of our aircraft was the only order of business. We all had a job to do and most of us went about it with as much dedication and enthusiasm we could muster, no matter how tired and dirty we were. It was during one of these "flight-ops" when an incident occurred that could only result in my recognizing the intervening hand of God in a situation totally out of my control.

A flight deck is an incredibly organized yet busy, multi-task oriented part of an aircraft carrier, where it is an all-hands effort to defeat Murphy's Law: Whatever can go wrong will go wrong. Every activity is virtually choreographed, practiced and repeated to minimize damage to equipment and injury to personnel. But, inevitably, incidents do occur, especially during "night-ops." Returning aircraft are stopped (arrested) on the landing track, then, under direction of a "Yellow-Shirt," the pilot moves the plane off the track. Standard as well as operational procedure dictates a right-turn for aircraft being directed off the landing track. A high-thrust jet engine can blow anyone off the flight deck. On one particular occasion, I was that anyone.

For whatever reason, a "Yellow-Shirt" directed an RA-5 Vigilante aircraft off the landing track with a left turning maneuver. I was standing in what should have been a safe zone near the landing track preparing to receive one of our Squadron's F-8 Crusader aircraft that was returning to the ship from an earlier launch. I had just stowed my gear and as I turned back toward the landing track I was struck full blast by the jet wash of the Vigilante. I was knocked down and blown rather abruptly across the Flight Deck. And, as quickly as it happened, it was over. I didn't have time to be fearful or even excited. (All that came later). I had been caught in the jet blast and on my way over-board when I was stopped by a special piece of yellow equipment.

Here's the reality of that moment. That special piece of yellow equipment was out of place. Had it not been there I would have been in the ocean. Unrecognized by me but not unknown to God, my life was spared. God intervened in that situation in a miraculous way. Years later I came to know this truth and affirm it now. He had plans for my life and He had protected, or preserved me in accordance with His plan.

Like many who have come to the Lord at a point well beyond childhood, my salvation experience is marked by an unforgettable event, produced in an unusual circumstance, by a most unique God. Since He knows me so well, God used a personal emergency in my life to not only attract, but hold my attention.

Paralyzed by an allergic reaction to penicillin, I was flat on my back in a hospital. (You know, God can, and sometimes does, see to it that "up" is the only direction in which you can look). On this particular day, my wife, who had already been with me in my hospital room, wasn't expected back until late the following afternoon. I was alone with my thoughts and not sure about anything, especially my future. Medication prescribed by my doctor had caused hallucinations and I had refused to take any more. My personal doctor was away for the weekend and his associate was to look in on me. Looking back today, what seems a bit foolish now, was extremely serious at the time.

My doctor's associate came by alright, but he wasn't too pleased to discover I had refused my medication. I saw this man only once, but he made a lasting impression. He was a large man. Capable of blocking the light out of any doorway in which he chose to stand. And there he was, in the doorway of my hospital room. Without coming into the room, he announced his presence with a large room-filling voice and said, "By refusing to take your prescribed medication you could die! I hope you will see your doctor on Monday morning." And with that, he left. Apparently bedside manner was not his gift. However, he did leave me with something to occupy my thoughts: "You could die" captured more than my imagination.

I had seen death up close during my time in military service. I even knew it would claim me someday. But at 27, married a little more than one year, with a whole life to live, "You could die" got my attention. Physically immobilized and alone, my wife away until late the next day, no nurse scheduled in to give medication, and my doctor gone until Monday; I faced that Saturday night with a whole new attitude.

Some testimonies get over-involved and become fairly explicit about life styles and such. Some paint pretty graphic pictures of how bad things were, and how much control Satan had on their lives. Attitudes and actions associated with my life were most assuredly not an exception, but I'm not into a program that gives the Devil equal or more time. Let me simply say I was on my way to Hell on that particular Saturday, and Christ met me right where I was, in that hospital room. I had never heard of a "sinner's prayer" but I am certainly a sinner and I was definitely praying. I didn't try to make a deal with God for Him to let me live so I could live my life for Him.

I simply came to God on His terms, asked forgiveness, surrendered my will to His and asked for another chance to live, period!

I had refused the hallucination causing medicine, so I wasn't experiencing some sort of a chemically induced vision. Christ came into my hospital room and I was personally ministered to by the greatest physician ever. My anxiety was replaced with peace and when sleep finally came to me that night my eternal security was no longer in question. When I awoke the next morning, the Holy Spirit brought to mind what had taken place during the night. I confirmed it in my spirit and as I was enveloped with the Baptism of the Holy Spirit, peace beyond understanding came over me. I was sure, that no matter what, I belonged to Christ.

Slowly would be an overstatement, but my life was changed. I was "Born Again and Spirit filled" and, as with my physical birth, I needed to grow. I just didn't know how. The Holy Spirit took care of that too.

Growth is relative to what you are fed and how much. I was missing many of my spiritual meals. Work, play, or any excuse would do. Too busy for God and stuff. And, stuff was getting all my attention. God said enough of stuff and allowed me to contract a severe case of viral hepatitis. No medication required—just time. The doctor said it would take rest and lots of it. And certainly, no stuff.

Time is one of those funny things in life. You never have enough. But when you have it on your hands, what do you do with it? Television can be an escape, but I consider daytime viewing a curse. I could stretch a daily read of the paper into an hour. A browse of all our old magazines was complete before the end of the first week. The mail came around one o'clock. That took care of another ten minutes, unless the Reader's Digest was in the delivery. Three hours later I was looking for next month's issue. Bored, helped along with the word "extremely," came close to describing my daily routine.

When I look back on this period in my life, it's easy to see the hand of God at work. But while it was happening there was a different understanding. There I was, as miserable as I can ever remember being and blaming God. Why would He do this to me? I just had to have an answer. And, as one might expect, it came.

How that particular copy of the Holy Bible got on top of our T.V. shall remain a mystery until and unless it is revealed later. My wife didn't put it there and our daughter was too small, and because of my illness, no one had been in the house. But there it was. I was confronted with what I now know to be one of those life changing opportunities. Unlike magazines, which I usually read from the back, I opened the Bible at the front and began, what I was sure would be the beginning of a rather dull activity. My reading commenced with, "In the beginning, God . . ." [1] Well I was certainly at the beginning, but what I didn't know then is that there is no end.

I read the whole book. Then I read it again. That was some years ago and I'm still reading it. In fact, God has blessed me with multiple copies of His Word in different translations and such, and well, it is just the best reading around. It is so important to our faith. And, isn't that a topic we could get into? Everyone has heard something about faith. You know, ". . . the substance of things hoped for, the evidence of things not seen." Well I didn't have any. Saving faith yes, but not "walking" faith. So God just used the Word and the power of the Holy Spirit to build mine up in the Lord.

Remember, I had viral hepatitis. The doctor said it was one of the most severe cases he had ever seen. He told me to expect being laid-up for at least six months, perhaps even a year. There was no medicine. All I could do was rest and give my body an opportunity to recover. In the process I came to the Word of God and my faith was gradually kindled from a burning ember to a leaping flame.

I prayed, my family prayed, saints in other parts of the country prayed, whole churches prayed, and evidently God was willing for me to be healed.

I had been to the doctor for the diagnosis. Returned for a two-week checkup and had lab work done to confirm one of the worst cases of viral hepatitis in the doctor's career, and sent home to rest. Two weeks later, four weeks into the process, I was back at the doctor's office. Thank God I wasn't worse, but I wasn't much improved either.

On my third trip, six weeks into the treatment and testing program, my visit was somewhat extended. The nurse came back for another blood sample. Said they needed to run more tests than they had anticipated. A little while later the doctor asked me into his office where he informed me that my blood count was normal, on both tests. He didn't know what I had been doing, but whatever it was, I should keep doing it.

Well, I have to say, praying for healing is one thing, but praying for healing and being healed is a tremendous faith builder. And it wasn't just my prayers, but the prayers of many who prayed, believing God, and I was healed.

Hours could be spent in relating just a few of the personal touches my family and I have received as we have grown closer and more dependent on the Lord. None of my circumstances or personal calamities have ever caught God by surprise. He has always been there. Even during the times in my life when I was unaware of His presence and most assuredly, during the time since I became a Believer.

When contemplating an event occurring in August 2012, my thoughts are quickly drawn to God's personal involvement in the steps associated with my life, preceding and immediately following the event. God's Word is direct and specific when it comes to the ordering of a man's steps. The Psalmist wrote these applicable words. "The Lord makes firm the steps of the man who delights in him; though he may stumble, he will not fall, for the Lord upholds him with his hand." [2] The Hebrew word for man in these verses is *gebër*, and means a certain or individual man. Not a "special person" but a man or woman who knows God and wants His will for and in their life.

God's ordered steps for my life have not always been easy or without stress. Around 5:00 a.m. on August 6, 2012, an elephant slipped into my room, put a rock on my chest and proceeded to sit on it. I experienced all the negative effects of a heart attack and awoke in Mercy Hospital suffering with congestive heart failure and with an angioplasty and a stint in my left arterial arteries. Definitely not the way I had planned to begin my work-week. Something I have probably said many times before but, "this" gave me cause to pause.

I was taken to the hospital emergency room and into an examination room where the magnitude of my situation was audibly exclaimed by the medical staff who were assessing and addressing my condition. All were in agreement that I was experiencing a heart attack and their actions were directed by protocol. They took control of the moment while my thoughts were gripped by the seriousness of the event. I went directly to God and submitted my personal understanding to Him that I wasn't done with what He had called me to do. I surrendered to His will and asked God if it was time for me to come home. His answer was immediate and the Holy Spirit simply said "No." It was so definite it seemed to be audible. I'm still amazed everyone in the room didn't hear it. Or, perhaps they did.

In any event I heard it and peace, His peace, took control. When the episode was complete, I woke up in an ICU room with renewed assurance that God was in charge and without doubt, none of this circumstance had caught Him by surprise. My thoughts drifted into revisiting some of the recent steps I now know God had ordered for my life.

Several weeks prior to the heart attack I had been mowing my lawn. Something I did as a matter of course for some physical exercise and the fact the yard needed to be mowed. Added to this understanding is the fact that I collect and compost the lawn clippings. Not a remarkable commitment but one that requires multiple "load-hauling walks" from the mower to the compost bin in the back yard. Usually twelve to fourteen trips per mowing effort. In reality, there was nothing extraordinary about it. However on that particular mowing adventure I ran over an exposed tree root and bent the blade on the mower. Unusual on this occurrence because I had pushed the mower over this same root many times before with no negative results.

A bent blade is unacceptable and a replacement was necessary. But, try as I might, I could not get the blade off of the mower. So I took the mower, blade on, to the shop and asked them to replace the blade. Later that day a shop rep called to tell me they had the blade off but in the process they had inspected the shaft and it was bent. He further explained the shaft was bent up inside the engine housing and because it was a "short shaft" the problem was not an easy fix. He also told me the cost to repair the engine exceeded the value of the mower. So, how does this relate to God ordering my steps?

It all came together pretty well when I understood that in previous years I had easily removed the blade for sharpening. This year I could not get it off of the mower. Had I been able to remove the blade on my own, I would have simply replaced it and "banged on" with a bent shaft. All while my as yet undiscovered heart condition grew worse during the warmest season of the year. So, instead of mowing, bagging and hauling, composting, and trimming, God made my lawn mowing activities a "not at this time" thing which removed me from the process and an eminent probability of succumbing to the heat and exhaustion as a result of my heart condition. Ordered steps.

God also has a few specific things to say about a man providing for his family. In his first letter to Timothy, Paul wrote, "Anyone who does not provide for their relatives, and especially for their own household, has denied the faith and is worse than an unbeliever." [3]

Our household was fiscally running in the negative column each month as a direct result of the national economy and its impact on real estate development. Projects upon which I relied for funds to augment our standard SSI income were defunded and stopped. It was obvious some type of employment would be necessary to assist meeting our normal monthly financial obligations. For whatever the reasons prospect after prospect went to no or not at this time. In early December, 2011, I was made aware of a potential position with a time-share resort company in Branson, MO. Just before Christmas I interviewed with that company. The immediate follow-up was uneventful and resulted in another not at this time response.

In mid-January, 2012, I had a follow-on meeting with a representative of that company and was encouraged to re-contact them. I did and in mid-February, 2012, I interviewed with another representative of that company. Good and bad resulted. Good: I was accepted for employment. Bad: The representative with whom I would be working dropped out of the mix. I was put on hold. In late February, 2012, I was re-contacted by another of the company's representatives and asked to come in for an interview. Result: I was hired and went to work on March 12, 2012. Ordered steps.

While I was doing all this I continued to search-out employment with some local proprietors and national franchise companies. No response from any station. After March 12, 2012, it was of little or no concern. It had always been my intention to secure "part-time" employment. None were available for me. So, full-time in Branson became the basis of my employment. Again, ordered steps.

Our family had been without medical insurance for several years. As a full-time employee, I became eligible for an employer sponsored group health plan. With a 120 day qualification period my start date became very important to the schedule of as yet unforeseen events. The company extended their formal offer to sign-on for their major medical insurance on July 9, 2012. Following a review and some detailed discussions with my wife, we accepted and the proposed insurance went "in-force" on July 20, 2012. Had I not been allowed to start during the month of March, 2012, this insurance would not have been available or in-force on August 6, 2012. Ordered steps.

Preforming the work associated with my position involved tours which required long walks on-property for each tour. Sometimes three tours per day. Normally that was not an issue with me or a potential customer. Sometimes though, a customer "required" transportation via a golf-cart to accomplish a tour. From commencement of my work in Branson I had missed no scheduled work days. During the last three weeks prior to the event of August 6, 2012, I was responsible for thirteen tours. Nine on-property tours were required. Four customers were on-property guests and had no need for a walking-tour. Of the nine customers actually requiring an on-property tour, for reasons obvious and not, all required transportation via a golf-cart. So, instead of "long walks" during the heat of the day, I toured via a golf-cart. This was a blessing for me because I was experiencing some shortness of breath during those three weeks. With little imagination it would not be difficult seeing myself succumbing to some type of physical malady, perhaps a heart attack or stroke during a walking-tour. Ordered steps.

Instead of being on the road to or from, or actually in Branson, on the day of the event, I was at home in Springfield with my wife when the heart attack occurred in the early hours of the day. Our home is only blocks from Mercy Hospital ER. Ordered steps.

I walked into the ER at Mercy Hospital and just as I was collapsing out of the arms of my wife, someone slid a wheel chair under me and I was off, down the corridor to the examining room. Ordered steps.

The medical staff in the ER examination room quickly made the call without going through a battery of tests and declared my condition as a heart attack and I was prepped for immediate surgery. The cardiovascular surgeon was on-site and ready to perform in the operating room within minutes of my arrival. Ordered steps.

Totally out of my conscious understanding, but not God's, the surgeon quickly set to work, discovered the situation and took the necessary steps to correct the problem. I was operating with 10% heart function as a result of congestive heart failure. With the surgical improvements in place I advanced to 25% heart function, with an irregular heartbeat. I awoke in that condition in an ICU room where I was scheduled for an additional treatment to correct the arrhythmia. The treatment was unsuccessful and I was sent to a regular room in the hospital to await further developments.

Around 3:00 a.m. the next morning I was told by the attending nurse that my "sinus rhythm" was normal. Somewhere between 11:00 p.m. and 2:00 a.m. God reached down, touched my heart and it returned to a normal heartbeat. Ordered steps.

With the exception of blood pressure medications during the past three years, prescription drugs have never been part of my life. As a new "heart patient," that was no longer the case. While in the hospital I was administered more than thirteen drugs every day. Eleven came in the morning followed by the remaining two in the evening. Results from this onslaught of medication were an extremely sore stomach and hallucinations of gargantuan proportions. These conditions interfered with sleep and normal food consumption. The hallucinations invaded every part of my room and mind. The answer was the Word of God, where I went with the aid of the Hospital's in-room Gideon Bible. Hours were spent in the chair near my bed in prayer and immersion into the Word. Getting close to the Lord was very rewarding and provided the best way to deal with the demons that were covering the room. The stomach problem was another situation.

My doctor's decision was to have a sonogram performed on my stomach and GI track. Results were inconclusive, but they did determine my Gallbladder was swollen and inflamed. Had the meds not made my stomach hurt the condition with my Gallbladder would have gone undetected and put more strain on my weakened heart. They took away some of the meds and added two that were specifically designed to help with the Gallbladder situation. Ordered steps.

On the day we left the hospital, eight days after the event, we had to collect the prescribed medications from our pharmacy. Everyone knows heart meds are expensive and we knew it would be challenging for us as well. Along with some new pieces of equipment, these new meds would be expensive. When we came to the counter to collect our order, we were pleasantly surprised to discover our "drive-out" price had been dramatically impacted by the Rx provision in our medical insurance. This is the insurance that became in-force as a result of my position with the Branson, MO company. Instead of the full price for each medication, we paid only a co-op portion which was very affordable. Ordered steps.

My medical team is committed to my wellbeing and they require periodic checks along with some post-operative tests to confirm my progress. They also prescribed a 36-session cardio-rehab program for me which involved three sessions per week with an option to follow-up on my own in a continuing phase program. I exercised the option and continue the process weekly. My work-outs consist of multi-apparatae, resistance-type muscle-training machines, along with some fairly strenuous cardio-vascular exercise activities. A team of physical therapists monitor my activities and encourage my effort. They tell me on a regular basis that no one with congestive heart failure can walk-through the tri-weekly program at the levels I have attained. Only with God's enablement. Ordered steps.

About five months into the post-operative program we were involved with a regular scheduled prayer service at our church. During this service, our Pastor and another brother in Christ were made aware of my situation and came to my side for specific prayer. Our Pastor prayed specifically for my healing and through the power of the Holy Spirit and mercy of the Lord, I felt the healing come into my heart. Ordered steps. I accepted and received it and can only say, "God is tremendous."

As affirmation of what the Lord did on my behalf, a specialized test to monitor my heart's condition indicated my heart infraction level was now at 34%. My cardiology team of physicians concluded that there is no longer a need to consider an implanting of a 24/7 defibrillation unit. Again, ordered steps.

Without doubt, God has been involved in and with every circumstance associated with the event of August 6, 2012. Through it all I have reaffirmed my dependence on His grace and His provision during the process. My commitment to serve Him has been renewed and made more paramount in my life. By releasing everything associated with the event to God I have grown in faith. His Word sets the facts in place. In his first general epistle, Peter wrote, "Humble yourselves, therefore, under God's mighty hand, that He may lift you up in due time. Cast all your anxiety on Him because He cares for you." [4]

God has led me to a total commitment resulting in my having turned over my work, my career, my family and my life to Him. He has given me a boldness to share the truth of our Living Savior with anyone the Holy Spirit directs.

He has met us in our darkest hour with the light of hope and the means to co-exist with, or rise above specific situations. When I realize how truly blessed and fortunate I am to have a personal relationship with Jesus Christ, words fail me. When I pause for this awareness, I am drawn to His Word. And there, as if written in bright neon, day-glow orange ink, is His personal call on my life:

> God said, ". . . rise, and stand upon thy feet: for I have appeared unto thee for this purpose, to make thee a minister and a witness both of these things which thou hast seen, and of those things in the which I will appear unto thee;" [5]

I am truly born again and filled with the Holy Spirit. God has called me out and made me an Evangelist for the Lord Jesus Christ. He has given me boldness beyond what I could ever have expected. My work provides many opportunities to share my enthusiasm for witnessing with others. My ministry is called "Faith Harvest." It is good to remember that in His Word, God said ". . . you have been saved, through faith—and this not from yourselves, it is the gift of God—." [6] It's God's work. We are the laborers in His field, ". . . look at the fields! They are ripe for harvest." [7]

I continue to pray for those occasions when God allows me to be in a particular place at a particular time when I am afforded an opportunity to encourage others to share the marvelous truth of how Christ is always available to anyone who asks Him to become part of their life.

May I leave you with this thought: God's Word is true: Salvation is truly a "Faith Harvest."

BIBLIOGRAPHY

God Saved Me, Bibliography by Chapter

Unless noted otherwise, all scripture verses are from the New International Version translation, Zondervan Bible Publishers, Grand Rapids, MI, © 1973, 1978, 1984, by International Bible Society, used by permission.

Introduction

1. Ephesians 2:8,9
2. John 4:35
   a. The Rise of the Religion of Antichristism
      David R. Mains
      Zondervan Publishing House, Grand Rapids, MI, 1985
   b. The Kingdom of the Cults
      Walter Martin
      Bethany Fellowship, Inc., Minneapolis, MN, 1977
   c. Ever Increasing Faith
      Smith Wigglesworth
      Gospel Publishing House, Springfield, MO,
      Revised Edition, 1971

Chapter One ~ Evangelism and the Local Church

Desire of the Local Body to be Involved

1. Titus 3.1-2
2. 1 Peter 3.15
3. Hebrews13.1-2
4. 1 Peter 5.5-6
5. Hebrews 5.6-10

6. Genesis 14.18
7. Psalm 110.4
8. Matthew 6.5-8
9. Matthew 6.9-13 *

   * King James Version, Published by the Syndics of the
   Cambridge University Press, Bentley House,
   200 Euston Road, London NW1 2DB

10. 2 Timothy 2.2

Local Body Must Make Itself Available

11. Acts 2.41-46
12. 2 Corinthians 9.5
13. Hebrews 3.13

Work Must be Grounded in the Local Body

14. Hebrews 10.23-25
15. 1 Peter 2.12
16. 1 Peter 1.1,2
    a. Calm Answers for a Confused Church
       Charles R. Swindoll
       Insight for Living, Fullerton, CA, 1988

"Lone Ranger" Evangelism is Not Required

17. Ephesians 5. 21
18. Acts 14.26
19. Hebrews 13.2
20. Ephesians 4.14-16
21. Ephesians 6.18

First Century Church / New Testament Church

22. Acts 14.26,27
23. Romans 8.9
24. Acts 15.2

Many are Called. Few Respond

25. Ephesians 4.11
26. Acts 1.8
27. 2 Corinthians 5.20
    b. Hand Me Another Brick
        Charles R. Swindoll
        Thomas Nelson, Inc., Nashville, TN, 1978

Fear and Confusion. Tools of the Devil

28. 2 Timothy 1.7
29. Matthew 28.19
    c. Fear of Witnessing
        Henry Morris
        Institute for Creation Research

Where are the Christians?

30. Galatians 5.19–21
31. James 1.23,24
    d. The Best of A. W. Tozer
        Compiled by Warren W. Wiersbe
        Baker Book House Company, Grand Rapids, MI, 1974

Hell is Promised to the Lost

32. 2 Thessalonians 1.7-9

33. Matthew 13.47-50

34. Hebrews 9.27

35. Revelation 20.11-15

   e. The Biblical Description of Hell

      Kathy A. Smith

      fillthevoid.org/Christian/Hell/Hellbiblicaldescription.html

   f. Heaven

      Randy Alcorn

      Eternal Perspective Ministries, 2004

Statement of Concern

36. Romans 3.9-12

37. Romans 1.21,22

   g. The Battle For The Mind

      Tim LaHaye

      Fleming H. Revel Company, Old Tappan, NJ, 1980

   h. The Best of A. W. Tozer

      Compiled by Warren W. Wiersbe

      Baker Book House Company, Grand Rapids, MI, 1974

   i. A Nation Without a Conscience

      Tim and Beverly LaHaye

      Tyndale House Publishers, Inc. Wheaton, IL 1994

   j. The Chaos of Cults

      Jan Karel Van Baalen

      Wm. B. Eerdmans Publishing Company, Grand Rapids, MI, 1953

Commitment to Each Other

38. James 2.17-19

Questions:

39. 2 Timothy 2.15-19

Chapter Two ~ Prayer, the Strength of Witness

Primary Principle

1. Colossians 4.2-4
2. Ephesians 6.18

God's Released Power

3. James 5.16
4. Romans 8.31
   a. The Power of Prayer and the Prayer of Power
      R. A. Torrey
      Kessinger Publishing Company, Whitefish, MT 2004

Praying in the Spirit

5. Acts 2.4
6. 1 Corinthians 14.15
7. Ephesians 6.18
8. Jude 1.20
9. 1 Corinthians 2.10-13
10. John 16.13-16
11. 1 Corinthians 14.26-28

For What Should We Pray?

12. Luke 10.2
13. Colossians 4.3
14. Acts 4.29
15. Ephesians 6.19
16. Colossians 4,4
17. 2 Thessalonians 3.1
18. Romans 10.1

19. 1 Timothy 2.1-8
   b. True Prayer—True Power
      Sermon by Charles H. Spurgeon
      at Exeter Hall, Strand, London, UK
      August 12, 1860

How Should We Pray?

20. Psalm 67.3
21. Psalm 50.14
22. James 5.16
23. 1 John 5.14,15
24. Matthew 21.22
25. Hebrews 11.1
26. 2 Chronicles 13.18
27. Ephesians 3.20
28. Psalm 31.24
29. 2 Corinthians 8.11

When Should We Pray?

30. Colossians 1.3
31. 1 Thessalonians 5.17
32. Psalm 55.17
33. Acts 16.25

For Whom Should We Pray?

34. John 17.9
35. James 5.13-16
36. 1 Thessalonians 5.25

What Should We Do at Our Local Church?

    37. John 15.5-8

Where Do We(I) Fit in All of This?

    38. Romans 8.16,17
        b. Enjoying Intimacy with God
            J. Oswald Sanders
            Moody Press, Chicago, IL, 1980

What Can We(I) Do?

    39. 1 Thessalonians 4.11-18
    40. Galatians 6.2-6
    41. Titus 1.8,9

What Will We(I) Do?

    42. James 1.5
    43. Psalm 27.14
    44. 2 Corinthians 9.3
    45. Acts 14.27
        c. *Ibid*

Questions

    46. 1 Corinthians 2.10-12

Chapter Three ~ The Word Is A Witness

Don't Leave Home Without It

    1. John 15.7
    2. John 15.16

Won't Return Empty (Void)

3. Isaiah 55.11
4. Romans 4.21
    a. You Mean the Bible Teaches That . . .
        Charles C. Ryrie
        Moody Press, Chicago, IL, 1974

Given to Us by God

5. 2 Timothy 3.16
6. 2 Peter 1.20,21
7. Psalm 102.18

Written for Our Benefit

8. Romans 15.4
9. 1 John 5.13,14
10. Romans 10.9–11

Explore and Learn What God Says

11. 1 Peter 3.15
12. 2 Timothy 2.15
13. John 8.31,32
14. 1 Corinthians 15.3,4
    b. The Bible and Tomorrow's News
        Charles C. Ryrie
        Victor Books, 1973

The Word as a Weapon Against Demonic Spiritual Forces

15. 1 Peter 5.8
16. Ephesians 6.10–18

17. Luke 4.4,8,12
18. Acts 16.17–18
    c. Secrets of a Prayer Warrior
        Derek Prince Ministries International
        Chosen Books, Grand Rapids, MI, 2009

Let the Word Speak, so You Can Speak to Others

19. Exodus 24.3,4
20. Acts 17.11

The Word Used to Build Up Our Spiritual Character

21. 1 Thessalonians 2.13
    d. You Can Make It
        Tom Williams
        Sword of the Lord Publishers, Murfreesboro, TN, 1988

The Word Can and Will be Tested

22. John 5.37–39
23. Luke 24.44–48
    e. Doctrine For Difficult Days
        J. Vernon McGee
        Thomas Nelson, Inc., Nashville, TN, 1996

Questions

24. Revelation 13.18
25. John 17.17
    f. Guidelines for the Understanding of the Scriptures
        J. Vernon McGee
        Thru the Bible Radio, Pasadena, CA, 1996

g. Evidence of Design
    Chuck Missler
    Taken from: *khouse.org/articles/1995/102/*

h. Archaeology and History Attest to the Reliability of the Bible
    Richard M. Fales, Ph.D.
    Taken from: *http://www.pinpointevangelism.com*

i. The Canonicity of the Bible
    Norman Geisler
    Ankerberg Theological Research Institute, 2005

j. Why We Have Confidence in the Bible
    Charles R. Swindoll
    Insight for Living, 2006

k. The Apocrypha, Canonicity of the Bible
    Relationship Between the Biblical and Extra-Biblical Writings
    Cutting Edge Ministries, 2008

l. More Evidence That Demands a Verdict, Preface, Page v
    Josh McDowell
    Campus Crusade for Christ, Inc. 1975

m. *Ibid*, Page 50

n. Guidelines for the Understanding of the Scriptures
    J. Vernon McGee
    Thru the Bible Radio, Pasadena, CA, 1996

o. The Best of A. W. Tozer
    Compiled by Warren W. Wiersbe
    Baker Book House Company, Grand Rapids, MI, 1974

Chapter Four ~ Fear and Guilt.
Satan's Convenient Ploy

What Did He Say to Eve?

1   Genesis 3.1-5

What Does That Make Him?

2. John 8.44

What Did Adam and Eve Do?

3. Genesis 3.6

Then What Did They Do

4. Genesis 3.7
5. Genesis 3.8

Why?

6. Genesis 3.10

Where Did That Leave Us?

7. Genesis 3.16
8. Genesis 3.17

What Did God Do?

9. Genesis 3.21-23
10. Genesis 3.24

Can We Identify with Adam and Eve?

11. Matthew 7.1
   a. Eve's Journey
      Nehama Aschkenasy
      Univ. Philadelphia Pr., Philadelphia, PA, 1986 (Not verbatim)
   b. Modern Manhood
      Damon Cinaglia

MARK INC Ministries, 2003 (Not verbatim)

c. Basic Bible Studies

Francis A. Schaeffer

Tyndale House Publishers, Wheaton, IL, 1976

What are Some "Current Lies" from Satan?

12. James 4.7

God Didn't Give Us a Spirit of Fear

13. 2 Timothy 1.7
14. Romans 8.31
15. Philippians 4.13
16. 1 John 4.15-18
17. Psalm 118.6

I Didn't Witness When I Should Have, Now I . . .

18. 2 Timothy 2.15
19. Matthew 10.42
20. Psalm 94.14
21. Hebrews 10.35
22. 2 Corinthians 4.8
23. Hebrews 13.5
24. Romans 8.28

Claim the Victory and Press On

25. Acts 14.27
26. 1 Peter 3.15
27. Ecclesiastics 7.8

Where Does God Say "We" Save Anyone?

28. John 6.65

Ol' What's His Name Will Do Anything

29. Romans 12.3
30. 1 Corinthians 14.33
31. Ephesians 6.11
32. Romans 8.28
33. James 4.7

Questions

34. Colossians 1.16
    d. History of Satan
       Gary Goodworth, *2003*
    e. The Origin of Satan
       From: angelfire.com/mi/dinosaurs/lucifer.html
    f. Doctrine For Difficult Days
       J. Vernon McGee
       Thomas Nelson Publishers, Nashville, TN, 1996
    g. Why Did God Create Satan?
       From: s6.invisionfree.com/Bible_Voice/ar/t41.html
    h. The Bible & Christianity
       From: evangelical.us/lds-church/jesus-lucifer-not-brothers.html
    i. God Doesn't Believe in Atheists
       Ray Comfort
       Living Waters Publications, Bellflower, CA

Chapter Five ~ Show Yourself Approved

You are Christ's Representative

1. 2 Corinthians 5.20
2. Romans 10.9

3. James 4.7
4. Proverbs 3.5
5. 1 Thessalonians 2.13
6. James 2.18
   a. Tell It Often Tell It Well
      Mark McCloskey
      Here's Life Publishers, Inc., San Bernardino, CA, 1985
      Know What God Says About:
7. Isaiah 53.6
8. Romans 3.10-12
9. Genesis 2.16,17
10. Romans 6.23
11. Romans 6.23
12. Jeremiah 49.12
13. John 4.24
14. Isaiah 45.21
15. Isaiah 44.6
16. 2 Peter 3.9
17. Romans 15.4
18. 2 Timothy 3.16,17
19. John 8.31,32
20. Isaiah 40.8
21. 1 John 5.13
22. John 1.1
23. Genesis 1.1
24. 1 Samuel 2.10
25. Isaiah 9.6
26. John 14.6
27. John 10.30
28. Hebrews 1.8
29. Isaiah 43.10,11
30. 1 John 2.1,2
31. Hebrews 11.1
32. Ephesians 2.8,9

33. 2 Corinthians 5.7

34. Romans 3.28

35. James 2.14-17

    b.   Hell's Best Kept Secret
        Ray Comfort
        Whitaker House, Springdale, PA, 1989

    c.   The Person and Work of the Holy Spirit
        René Pache
        Moody Press, Chicago, IL, 1954

Study—Pray—Study—Pray. You should:

36. 2 Timothy 2.15

37. Philippians 4.6

38. Ecclesiastes 7.25

39. 1 Thessalonians 5.17

    d.   The Practice of Godliness
        Jerry Bridges
        Navpress, Colorado Springs, CO, 1984

Be Ready

40. 1 Peter 3.15

Share the Experience

41. 1 Corinthians 15.1-4

Declare and Demonstrate the Fruit of the Spirit

42. Matthew 12.33, 35

43. Matthew 7.16-23

44. Ephesians 5.18

45. Galatians 5.16-18

46. Galatians 5.19–21
47. James 2.18
48. Galatians 5.22–25
  e. Essential Truths of the Christian Faith
      R. C. Sproul
      Tyndale House Publishers, Carol Stream, IL, 1992

Put It in Your Heart Where Your Mind Can Find It

49. John 18.9
50. John 10.27–30

Know Where You Are

51. Philippians 4.7

Know When to Quit

52. Titus 3.9–11

Sample Questions—Not Stock Spiel

53. Psalm 37.18
54. John 6.47
55. Colossians 2.5
56. Revelation 20.15
57. 1 Peter 2.24
58. Luke 16.22–31
59. John 14.6
60. Psalm 23.6
61. Romans 10.9
62. Ephesians 3.6
63. Titus 1.2
64. 1 John 5.20

65. 1 Corinthians 1.27

66. Colossians 1.10

67. 1 Corinthians 15.55

68. Matthew 13.42

69. Colossians 3.24

70. Revelation 21.1

71. 2 Peter 1.20,21

72. Acts 4.12

73. Proverbs 16.25

74. Jude 1.4

75. Romans 8.28-34

76. 2 Peter 3.9

Questions

77. John 1.41

    f.   Adam Hersh Posters

        Adam Hersh Company

        2012 Pierce Mill Road NW Washington, DC 20010

Chapter Six ~ Make Christ The Topic

Often a Difficult Thing to Do

1. Philippians 4.13

2. 1 Corinthians 3.11-15

3. 2 Timothy 1.7

    a.   Grace Notes

        Warren Doud

        1705 Aggie Lane, Austin, TX

A Natural Thing to Do

4. Philippians 4.13

5. Exodus 20.7
6. Ephesians 4.29
7. Ephesians 4.31
8. Philippians 4.8
9. 1 Peter 2.11
10. Exodus 20.17
11. Proverbs 14.12
12. Matthew 7.17
13. 1 Timothy 6.10
14. 1 Peter 4.10
15. John 15.17
16. Romans 12.9-10
17. 1 Corinthians 13.4-7
18. 1 Corinthians 13.13
19. Romans 12.3
20. Ecclesiastes 1.9
21. Psalm 107.2
22. 1 Corinthians 1.9

Let the Situation/Individual Set the Tone

23. 1 Peter 3.8
24. Psalm 14.27
25. Hebrews 4.12
26. Matthew 9.35-36
27. 1 Peter 3.8
28. Matthew 5.11,12
    b. The Compassion of Jesus
       A Sermon Delivered by
       C. H. Spurgeon
       At Metropolitan Tabernacle, Newington. UK
       Published December 24, 1914.

29. John 20.27
    c. The Gospel According to Jesus
       John F. MacArthur, Jr.
       Academie Books, Zondervan Publishing House,
       Grand Rapids, MI, 1989

Opportunities to Make Christ the Topic

30. 1 Peter 3.15
31. Nahum 1.7
32. Matthew 5.45
    d. The Measure of a Church
       Gene A. Getz
       Regal Books, Glendale, CA 1976

How Do You Do It?

33. Romans 7.15
34. John 21.17
35. 2 Peter 1.20,21
36. Genesis 19.26
    e. Evangelism Explosion III International *Paraphrased*
       P O Box 23820 Ft. Lauderdale, FL
    f. J. Vernon McGee,
       Through The Bible Radio Pasadena, CA

Questions

37. John 20.29
38. Genesis 1.26
39. 2 Corinthians 13.14
40. Revelation 3.20

41. Acts 11.26
42. Exodus 20.3
43. Genesis 17.21
44. Genesis 17.20
    g. Pantheism's Concept of God's Omnipresence
        Tim Temple
        From: *livingbiblestudies.org/printable/study/TT45/008.htm*

Chapter Seven ~ Wrap It Up. Give It Away

1. John 10.10

What's in a Gift Box?

2. 1 Peter 3.15
3. Psalm 145.17-19
4. Hebrews 10.23
5. Revelation 3.20
6. Jeremiah 23.24
7. Romans 7.5
8. 2 Corinthians 5.17
9. John 15.16

How Do You Wrap It?

10. Hebrews 11.1
11. Romans 10.13
12. John 5.24
13. Galatians 2.20
14. John 10.27

Why Wrap It Anyway?

15. John 3.16

4. 1 Peter 5.6-7
5. Acts 26.16 *

   * King James Version, Published by the Syndics of the
   Cambridge University Press, Bentley House,
   200 Euston Road, London NW1 2DB

6. Ephesians 2:8, 9
7. John 4:35

GOD SAVED ME